MAKE 'EM LAUGH

35 Years of the Comic Strip, the Greatest Comedy Club of All Time!

JEFFREY GURIAN AND **RICHIE TIENKEN**

INTRODUCTION BY **CHRIS ROCK**

Skyhorse Publishing

Skyhorse Publishing books may be purchased in bulk at special discounts for sales
promotion, corporate gifts, fund-raising, or educational purposes. Special editions can
also be created to specifications. For details, contact the Special Sales Department,
Skyhorse Publishing, 307 West 36th Street, 11th Floor, New York, NY 10018
or info@skyhorsepublishing.com.

Skyhorse® and Skyhorse Publishing® are registered trademarks of Skyhorse
Publishing, Inc.®, a Delaware corporation.

Visit our website at www.skyhorsepublishing.com.

10 9 8 7 6 5 4 3 2 1

Library of Congress Cataloging-in-Publication Data

Gurian, Jeffrey L. Make 'em laugh : 35 years of The Comic Strip, the greatest comedy
club of all time! / Jeffrey Gurian and Richie Tienken ; introduction by Chris Rock.
      p. cm.

ISBN 978-1-62087-074-7 (hardcover : alk. paper)
1. Comic Strip (New York, N.Y.) 2. Comedians–United States–Anecdotes.
I. Tienken, Richie. II. Title.
PN3166.N4C66 2012
792.7'6097471–dc23

                              2012027236

Printed in the United States of America

CONTENTS

FOREWORD BY RICHIE TIENKEN

Even as I'm writing this book, it's hard for me to believe that thirty-five years have gone by since we first opened the doors of The Comic Strip on June 1, 1976.

Coming from a simple background and leaving home at fourteen to make my way in the world, I realize life was not set to absolutely wind up the way it did.

Somehow, I went from owning six bars in The Bronx to managing one of the biggest stars in the comedy world: Eddie Murphy. When I think about it now, honestly, I still can't quite figure out how it all happened. But I'll tell you one thing: It was quite a trip!

I've gone from having all of my money stolen by a shady contractor (while trying to build The Strip—until, at the last second, my landlord stepped in to save the day) to breaking ties with my former client Eddie Murphy, which interestingly enough led to me meeting and marrying my wife, Jeannie, and having my two sons, Jonathan and Richie. Over and over, experiences that started out negative turned into something more positive than I could ever imagine. And it all has been more than I ever could have hoped for.

How do you wrap your mind around the fact that you helped launch the careers of people like Jerry Seinfeld, Chris Rock, Ray Romano, Eddie Murphy, George Wallace, and Adam Sandler? It's still inconceivable to me, but when Jeffrey and I did the interviews for the book, every comic said The Strip was his home, and they all were grateful for the support—particularly for my personal support.

A few years ago, I went through a serious medical crisis and had to be away from the club for a while. Thanks to God, to the support of my wife and kids, and to those around me, I came through it and was able to come back to this club that has been my life for so long.

I want to take this opportunity to thank my good friend and coauthor Jeffrey Gurian for helping me tell my story and the stories of all the people who came through here during the past thirty-five years. That's all I'm gonna say about him right now, 'cause I thank him again in the acknowledgments.

In closing, I just want to express my gratitude for all the good things that life has given me, and even for the not so good things. It's all been part of my path and what led me to where I am now.

Life has taught me many lessons. Some great, some not so great, but it's been a spectacular ride, and it ain't over yet!

I'd like to dedicate this book to my sister, Joanie, who was like the mom of the club if there was to be one; to my wife, Jeannie, and to my kids, Jonathan, Richard, Jacqui, Dawn Marie, and Christina; and to my grandchildren, Giovanna, Vincent, Brittany, Taylor, and Brayden.

Richie Tienken

June 2012

FOREWORD BY JEFFREY GURIAN

This book represents four years of work. Hard work! I started it in the summer of 2008 at the Just for Laughs Festival in Montreal by interviewing Larry Miller, George Wallace, and Paul Provenza. Since then, it's taken on a life of its own and has become a labor of love for me. It's made me kind of the historian of the most legendary comedy club ever, The Comic Strip.

When I started writing comedy at the age of twelve, there was no possible way for me to know that I would someday have the opportunity to tell the stories of so many people who changed the face of comedy not only in this country, but all over the world.

I'm very grateful to my pal Richie Tienken for trusting me to tell his story and the stories of others in this book. It's been an amazing ride and more fun that I could have imagined.

Not only am I grateful for the opportunity to do this book, but I'm grateful to have become part of The Comic Strip family, because that's what it is . . . a family. I feel like I have a second home there. I've spent more time at The Strip during the last four years than anywhere else.

I come in and see J. R. by the bar in his ever-present blue shirt, and I know I'm home.

I've taken more meetings in the tiny former coatroom that passes for Richie's office than I could ever imagine. Once with Ray Romano, we had five men in there, in a space that's already too tight when you're alone!

My history with The Strip goes back a long time. I sat in that little room many years ago with Lucien Hold, who was the face of The Comic Strip for twenty-five years. Many people thought he owned it, and Richie never minded that.

Lucien was always very kind to me, to the point where he once set up the video system in the club so I could do a comedy news broadcast from the stage during one of the shows, and everyone there said, "Lucien must really like you, 'cause he doesn't do that for anyone."

Years later, I sat with him in that tiny office and tried to alleviate the pain he was living with from scleroderma (which finally killed him) by doing spiritual healing on him. He was open to it and told me that it helped.

The Strip has changed my life as well. It's allowed me to start performing stand-up, which was a dream of mine for many years, and now I actually host shows there every week. It also allowed me to produce a benefit for diabetes, which took my dad, Raymond Gurian, back in 2001.

I'd like to dedicate my part of the book to my mom and dad, Marge and Ray Gurian, who gave me my sense of humor; to my daughters, Elizabeth DeRobertis and Kathryn Siry, who have had to put up with my sense of humor; and to their gorgeous children, Nicky, Lilly, Brookie, and Adrienne, to whom I'm simply Poppa Jeff! And that's my greatest gift!

Enjoy the book!

Jeffrey Gurian

June 2012

INTRODUCTION BY
CHRIS ROCK

I didn't go to college, and I regret it. Every now and again I have a conversation with somebody and they use a reference like Cantinflas or a word like deciduous, and I get that ol' GED feeling. I'm smart, but I have a hole in my knowledge, like a superhero with arthritis. I don't know a lot of sociology or economics, but I do have a lot of opinions about sociology and economics—good if you want to be a comedian; bad if you want to be the comedian's accountant. But don't think I didn't learn anything. Far from it. For the job I wanted, I couldn't have picked a better school than The Comic Strip. For one thing, you didn't need a Pell Grant. I got in straight from Red Lobster.

It's true. Comedy clubs are colleges for comics. Especially the New York ones. Especially back in the eighties. The two main schools (and schools of thought) were Catch a Rising Star and The Comic Strip. Catch was Yale, and the Strip was Illinois State University, Urbana. Catch was stressful, like you were always on the verge of being expelled if you didn't keep up your grades. The Strip was laid back. If you put in the work and studied, you would do well. But if you blew off a term smoking pot, it didn't go on your permanent record. Catch was more rigorous, like you needed to back up your joke with references. The Strip was like, "fooood fiiiight!"

(And it was frowned upon to be enrolled in both schools, though some people had waivers.)

I was basically a Strip guy. Our faculty were the waitresses, talent coordinator Lucien Hold, and owner Richie Tienken. Lucien was a tall, patrician fellow with searing eyes and a Three Musketeer's mustache, who called everybody "Mister" in an upper-crust accent, as in "five minutes, Mister Rock." He probably never had a mouse in his apartment unless the mouse had an ascot. Richie Tienken was the white-haired part-owner of the Strip. He managed a lot of major comedians, but he was approachable. He had powerful shoulders and was genial, like a bouncer who babysat on the side. They served as good cop (Richie)/ bad cop (Lucien). Or good president/bad dean. Richie probably could afford to be nice because he was—like his name—rich-ie. He gave advice like, "Keep it clean young man; you'll last longer." (He called everybody "young man," even Laura Kightlinger.) Lucien couldn't be "nice" because part of his job was deciding which comedians got onstage and which ones went home plotting his death. But Lucien was a great guy once you got to know him. He was charming in a weird way, like a guy who was really chatty after he'd just woken up in a morgue.

We didn't have fraternities at The Strip. Our version of hazing was bumping the younger guys. A young kid would be offstage in The Strip's little ante-chamber, eager to hit the stage because it was Saturday night second show, also known as the best audience of the week show, the one to record the tape that would lead to the Letterman spot. Leaning forward like a track star at the starting line, the young kid would be hearing the countdown in his head: "Three . . . two . . . hey, who just tapped me on the shoulder? Is that Robin Williams going past me?" Then the kid had to sit down for two hours, while Robin worked out his latest HBO special. But it was fair because one day that kid would be the bumper and someone younger and newer would be the bumpee. I got bumped by all the greats. Alan Colmes. Joe Bolster. Gilbert Gottfried.

Our school had boosters, too. People who weren't enrolled but showed up at The Strip regularly, like welterweight boxer Mark Breland, Asperger-syndrome comedian Tiny Tim, and heavyweight rapper LL Cool J. Nothing worse than getting heckled by LL Cool J. He was bigger than everybody, and his heckles rhymed.

And what school could call itself an institution of higher learning without a sports team? We had The Comic Strip softball team whose record was something like 0–1,000. It's hard to root for your team when you're getting your ass kicked regularly by the Friar's Club and the Actor's Studio. But I rooted for them anyway.

Watching other comedians could teach you a lot. There was one guy named Charlie Barnett who worked the streets putting down a hat for tips. But every now and again he would come inside (when it rained) and work The Strip, where he made less money. He was a visiting professor. He taught us how important it is to control an audience by giving off confidence. This was undoubtedly the result of having to work a crowd in the street who had access to rocks. One night, Charlie Barnett got a red light, which meant he had five minutes left. Charlie, used to being outside, didn't use a microphone when he was on at The Strip. He just projected to the rear of the house. At the five-minute light, he turned his back on the audience and started yelling a slew of old jokes, but the best old jokes ever written, jokes that had brought tears to the eyes of Moses. As he fired off one joke after the other like T-shirts from an air gun, the audience exploded with every punch line. With one minute left, Charlie walked off the stage through the crowd, backwards. He kept firing off jokes as he went, with the audience gasping for air. Finally, he reached the back of the house, told the last joke, the audience erupted, exactly five minutes were up, and he exited the room. That's confidence!

In a different manner, we learned timing from professors like Dennis Wolfberg who really had been a teacher in a former life. He is the only comedian I've ever seen who never bombed. Not only that, but he was the funniest person I ever saw in a twenty-minute stretch. He had a very peculiar but effective way of delivering a joke, by stuttering into the punchline. The combination of the stutter, his bulging eyes, his manic expression, his wild Einstein hair, and the punchline itself would rock the audience every time. There was something about that deliberate stutter, not really a stutter, but a fumbling-to-get-the-word-out tic that delayed the payoff just long enough to always make the audience scream. And that stutter-tic definitely increased the loudness of the reaction by at least 30 percent. Same joke without the tic, 30 percent less laughs, no doubt. Subtleties like that are what made the great comedians the great comedians.

Professor Wolfberg was a master of timing.

We also had the guys who were professional students, i.e. (I have no idea what i.e. means.) the guys who never left the school. They always came up with a new reason to do another semester—either out of a love of the campus or just being crazy. These guys never changed a word of their acts, and why should they? The audience is supposed to be new, not the jokes. People like D. F. Sweedler, Stu Trivax, and Howard Feller.

And like every school, our college had upperclassmen: Jon Hayman. Jerry Seinfeld. Carol Leifer. Larry Miller. George Wallace. Joey Vega. And Paul Reiser.

Then there was my class: Colin Quinn. Adam Sandler. Jeff Garlin. Ray Romano. Jeff Stilson. Eddie Brill. Susie Essman. And Jon Stewart.

And then the underclassmen: Louis CK. Wanda Sykes. Dave Attell. And Sarah Silverman.

My graduation—not long after my father passed—was when I was picked right from the stage of The Comic Strip to be on *Saturday Night Live*, which turned out to be my grad school.

It was also the same trajectory as my hero who had been the big man on campus at The Strip and, let's be real, the person who put The Comic Strip on the map—Eddie Murphy.

So, you are about to read about my higher institution of learning, The Comic Strip, a place that I adored then and now. So, yes, I didn't go to "college" college, but it's the best decision I ever made—and one that my daughters are forbidden to repeat.

There's the bell. Get to class.

Chris Rock

INTRODUCTION
TO THE COMIC STRIP

In 1975, there were two comedy clubs in all of Manhattan: Budd Friedman's Improv on West 44th Street, which he opened in 1963; and Rick Newman's Catch A Rising Star, which didn't come along until 1972.

But if it hadn't been for a Bronx bartender named Tony D'Andrea, who had a knack for doing impressions, there might never have been a third club called The Comic Strip. Tony was working at a bar called The Bull and Bush for a guy named Richie Tienken, who had been in the bar business all his life. D'Andrea, who was intent on performing a set at Catch A Rising Star, invited his boss to come down and watch him. Monday nights in the Bronx were always slow, and that just happened to be the night when D'Andrea was scheduled to perform. So, Tienken came down with a bunch of others to give D'Andrea moral support.

The first thing that struck Tienken was the size of the Catch crowd on a Monday night. "They were three deep at the bar, and business looked great," Tienken later recalled. But when midnight struck and D'Andrea hadn't yet gone onstage Tienken began to worry that his friends would be too drunk to stay much longer without creating a scene. They were Bronx residents not widely known for having patience.

Tienken encouraged D'Andrea to approach Rick Newman, Catch's owner, and tell him he had fourteen people waiting to see him and ask what time he would go on.

Newman's answer was startling: "I'm not concerned about customers. You'll go on when it's time for you to go on."

Tienken was intrigued and started coming down on a regular basis. He wasn't watching the comedy as much as he was watching how the place was run. For the next couple of weeks, he came almost every night. After about a month, he told his partner John McGowan, who had been partners with him in The Bronx, that they should look into opening a club in Manhattan. The seed was planted.

Now let's let Richie Tienken take over the story.

***

Once John and I decided to open a club, we needed someone in show business as a partner. Another Bronx bar owner named Marty Sheridan knew Bob Wachs, an entertainment lawyer in Manhattan, and he introduced us to Bob.

En route to our first meeting with Bob, as John and I drove down Second Avenue, I said, "You know, what we need is a place that was already a bar, 'cause that means that all the structure and the plumbing are in, and it'll make it a lot easier for us. Plus, it'll probably have a big room around the bar that we can use for a stage and audience."

So now we're heading downtown, and I'm on the passenger side looking out the window. I'll never forget this moment 'cause I'm talking to John, I'm looking at the stores, and he says to me, "Where are we gonna find a place like that?" And I said, as we got to the block between 81st and 82nd streets, "Right there! The Shannon Bar."

The bar was closed for business, but a sign in the window said the landlord lived around the corner. His name was David Eberhardt. He had a representative named Peter Dinkel and two brothers. David was the most helpful. Without them, there would have been no club.

The place was old—really old. But the bathrooms were in place, which meant that the plumbing was all in. There was no back room, but there was a big backyard. I asked the landlord's rep if he would rent the backyard too, and he said it came with it. I asked him who owned the building next door, in case I wanted to make the room even bigger, and he said Eberhardt owned that as well.

We continued on to Bob's office for our meeting. Bob went into a whole speech about show business, of which I knew nothing about, but *he* did, so that's good. That's what we wanted. After Bob listened to my *spiel*, he said, "That's all well and good, I have the connections, but what do we do about getting a place?"

I said, "We already did that. It's right here on Second Avenue. We'll have it open in a year." And it actually took a little more than a year, but we were really close.

Before we opened, Lucien Hold came in looking for a job. Someone had told him we needed a carpenter, and we hired him. When his job was finished, and we were getting ready to open, he was packing up his tools, and I asked him where he was gonna go. He was a dancer by trade, but there wasn't much work, so he thought he'd look for a job as a carpenter on Broadway. I said to him, "Why don't you work here as a bartender?" When he said he didn't know how, I said, "Lucien, if somebody asks for a beer, you give him a beer. That's bartending." And that's how Lucien became my bartender.

Bob Wachs and I alternated Mondays auditioning the talent. Comics Bob Nelson and Rob Bartlett, two white guys from Long Island, recommended that we look at their partner in The Identical Triplets, a young black kid also from Long Island named Eddie Murphy.

Nelson and Bartlett told Eddie to come in to the club, and he showed up on a night when Bob was working. Eddie came in not knowing our set up: that you wait to be told what time you're going up. So he went over to Wachs, 'cause he knows Wachs was in charge, and asked, "What time am I going up?" He thought he was going right up because he was an act already, not a newcomer. As a matter of fact, we later found out that he was almost insulted that we were watching him on newcomer night.

Wachs got mad at Eddie for questioning him. He told him, "You go up when I tell you to go up. And by the way, if you don't wanna go up, you can leave." Well, Eddie left, but when he told Nelson and Barlett what had happened, they told him to go back and talk to Richie Tienken.

I asked Bob what happened and why he threw Eddie out. Bob says, "I didn't like his attitude."

So I said he's coming in next Monday again, and I'll take a look at him. Eddie showed up very sheepish, and he called me "Mr. Tienken." I told him to call me Richie. He said, "Last week I was in, and I think I offended Mr. Wachs," and he told me the story. I replied, "Lookit, Eddie, I'm not saying yes or no. You go up onstage and I'll watch you, and then I'll decide. I don't like going against my partner, and I won't if I don't think you're worth it. But if I think you're worth it, I'll let you work here."

Eddie was very funny, but I would never knock Bob 'cause Bob's my partner. And I'm learning at that point that you stick with your partner, not with the acts. Loyalty was always very important to me.

So Eddie did his act and came offstage and asked, "What did you think?"

"Frankly, I thought you were very funny," I told him. Eddie asked, "Well, can we do anything? I'm sorry about what happened last week." I said, "You just call in your availability, and I'll get you spots." And that's how Eddie Murphy started at The Strip.

Later that year, Eddie asked me to be his manager. At first I turned him down. It wasn't until a week later that I accepted. I had never handled somebody's life before. I knew that in Eddie's mind, this was what he was going to do for the rest of his life. Although I had created businesses and opened bars, the thought of being responsible for someone's life just kind of scared me.

Turns out, his mother put him up to it. He had been telling her about me, and that he trusted me the most out of anyone, and she said, "So why don't you ask Richie to manage you?"

After I started thinking about it, I realized how complimentary it was that someone would think I was capable of handling his career and about a week later, I accepted his offer. And that's where Bob Wachs came in handy, 'cause Bob was an entertainment attorney.

When it came time for me to go to Hollywood with Eddie, I made Lucien my manager. That's when I started to let him book the shows. Before I let him do so, however, I needed to make sure he knew how to handle guys like Seinfeld, Larry Miller, and Paul Reiser. I used to sit with them all night if I had to. In the beginning, I went by what I thought was funny. Later on, I learned to go by what the audience thought was funny.

In those days, we used to let the comics do twenty-minute spots, but there was only so much time available. The comics' biggest complaint was, "How come I got to go on last night but not tonight?" I'd constantly have to explain to them that I was trying to be fair to everyone. Tuesday night was when Lucien and I worked on the lineup for the week. The comics had to let me know their "avails" by Tuesday afternoon. After that time, they'd all hang around me while I was working on the shows.

In those days, we had what was called "late night" for the guys who weren't that great yet. I always wanted to encourage those guys starting out 'cause they had more courage than I did to get up onstage at all. They were the ones I told to come back late at night. They went up in no particular order. Even if there were only six people in the audience, we still put people on.

Lucien called me one night, shortly before he died. He said, "Richie, I want to apologize to you. I know I'm not really doing my job lately." This is after twenty-five years. I'm like, "Doing your job? What are you talking about?" He says, "Well, I don't come in like I should." I said, "Lucien, it's okay. Don't worry about it. Are you booking the shows?" He said, "Oh yeah. Of course." I said, "That's fine, then don't worry, you're doing your job."

He said, "Richie, you always treated me good. If there's anything I can ever do for you, you tell me." So I said, "There's one thing I need you to do for me. I know I've never told you to do anything, but this time I'm telling you…" "Whatever you want, Richie. You tell me." I said simply, "Don't die." He says, "I'm trying not to."

Two weeks later, Ross Bennett, Lucien's best friend, calls me. He said, "Rich, I'm sorry to have to tell you this, but Lucien passed away last night." That was November 22, 2004.

Lucien always wanted to have a name for himself. I used to tell him, "Lucien, your name is bigger than The Comic Strip. You ask someone in California about The Comic Strip, they don't know. You mention Lucien from The Comic Strip, they know you."

Lots of people even thought he owned the club. I never cared if people thought that. I was managing Eddie Murphy, what did I care?

Everybody loved Lucien. Well, not everybody. He could be tough, too. He was very critical of the comedians. But he always meant well, and he was a great guy, which was proven by the size of the crowd that showed up at the memorial service we held for him at a Universalist Church on the West Side. Even I spoke, which I don't often do, and the church was packed.

Over the past thirty-five years, The Strip has had many people come through its doors—many comics just trying to get their few minutes on stage to extract laughs from the audience. What better way to memorialize the club's illustrious history and its impact on the lives of many in this tough business than through the words of those who've stood on its stage and made a whole lot of people laugh? In the pages that follow, you'll hear about the club's start, its stars, its owners and bartenders, and its legacy as *the* place to be if a career in stand-up is what you are after.

CHAPTER **ONE**

THE OLDER KIDS

When we were working out the structure of this book, we decided to make each chapter as if it was about a family, because The Comic Strip is just like a family—a family consisting of all dads, that is. This family consists of the parents, the older kids, and the younger siblings, as well as family friends and the next generation to come. The older ones, about whom this section is dedicated, are the ones who came along at the birth of The Comic Strip, starting with Jerry Seinfeld, and his crew: Paul Reiser, Larry Miller, George Wallace, and others.

Jerry Seinfeld[1]

Jerry Seinfeld is a comedian, actor, writer, TV and film producer, and director who made his name part of our lexicon with the eponymously named *Seinfeld*. The show ran from 1989 to1998. Since then, Jerry has co-written and co-produced *The Bee Movie*, directed Colin Quinn's *Long Story Short* on Broadway, and created the NBC show *The Marriage Ref* starring Tom Papa.

---

[1] The club officially opened for business on June 1, 1976, and Jerry came in to audition on June 17. His very first

When did you start performing, and what were some of your earliest memories of The Comic Strip?

Well, this is funny, because I actually started performing in my last semester of college. In order to finish college, I cooked up an independent study in stand-up comedy to get twelve credits so I could finish school and graduate. I had already done three-and-a-half years, and I figured, "Well, I might as well finish it. My parents'll be feeling better if I finish it, but I really was done with it, and I just wanted to go into stand-up comedy.

So I cooked up this thing, like a thesis, and I went to the theater department head, and I said, "Well, I wanna do a study on stand-up comedy, and I'll spend nine hours a day writing and twelve hours a day performing, and I just made up this whole crazy thing, and the funny thing is that Carol Liefer, who I had given it to when I knew her back from 1977, just sent it back to me a couple of weeks ago.

But I did it, so I didn't have to go to school for the last six months, so I could hang out here at The Strip and start doing comedy, and they went for it. They actually went for it and gave me the twelve credits, and that's how I graduated Queens College of the City University of New York in the summer of 1976.

I had been studying television production and drama and theater. Anything to do with show business was interesting to me. And somewhere in that period, from '74 to '75, I decided I was gonna do comedy.

I went to night school for a while in Queens, and I worked some construction jobs during the day, and I remember sitting on this ledge on Madison and 57th Street eating a sandwich—and it's still there that ledge. Now it's a Montblanc store. It was a bank at the time, and I remember sitting on this ledge watching people walk by and just trying to figure,

---

sign-up sheet is still hanging on the wall in the club and can be seen in this book as well. Jerry made the club his home and often talks about how he got started there and owes so much to Richie and the club, so it was very important to Richie to have Jerry in the book. We conducted the interview at the club, and Jerry showed up in a fantastic mood, ready to reminisce. He was open, honest, and forthright, and this is what he had to say.

"What is life? What are you supposed to do in life?" And the thought came to me: "What's the difference? Why don't I just do what I love to do . . . what I wanna do? And even if I'm a failure, it'll probably be a better life than anything else that I don't really wanna do." So in that moment I decided I'm gonna do comedy and I don't care what happens.

So, I really began performing early in '76. Maybe I did a couple of things in '75, when I was about twenty-one years old. And then I used to go to a couple of other clubs that were around at that time like The Improv, Catch A Rising Star, Pearl's Place on 96th Street. There was the Golden Lion Pub on 44th and Broadway, and I remember hanging around, and I swear I can remember it crystal clear. I remember standing at the bar at Catch and somebody was saying there's a new club opening on 2nd Avenue called The Comic Strip.

Do you remember your very first time onstage? Not at The Strip but just onstage doing comedy?

I do, and as a matter of fact I think my very first time onstage was at Catch. And it was probably the summer of '75. I got on the audition night line, and I got number one. They announced my name, and I went onstage and froze. I totally froze. I said a couple of things, and then I froze.

Elayne Boosler was the MC. I mentioned a couple of topics that I wanted to talk about, but that was all that came out. I had no idea that you really had to memorize what you wanted to say. I thought it was all gonna come out very easily.

I was on maybe two minutes, and then I just got off, and then she went on and said, "That was Jerry Seinfeld, the master of segue!" 'Cause I was just going, "My parents, the beach, driving . . ." I could only remember the topics I wanted to talk about, but I couldn't remember what I wanted to say about those things.

Then I didn't go back onstage again for probably about six months.

It must have taken a while to get over the embarrassment of that incident.

Not really. I didn't really do anything that night.

But weren't you embarrassed?

Yeah, I guess so. I still feel embarrassed a lot of the time. You gotta get over that.

So, I'm hanging out at Catch and I hear them say that The Strip just opened and they were looking for people. They said it was a lot easier to get on at The Strip, 'cause the place just opened. At Catch, it was really tough at that time, because we were starting from scratch and there were a lot of very established guys performing there regularly. They didn't really like giving up their stage time to newcomers.

So, I came over here, found out about the audition, drove here in the middle of the day, got onstage, and did five minutes. And Bob Wachs was in the audience, and they passed me right away on the audition.

You know, I was watching a movie the other day called *500 Days of Summer*, did you hear about it? It's a movie about this young guy who falls in love with this girl, and he becomes obsessed with the girl, and it's about the slow progress of the relationship, and then finally he sleeps with her. It's a very big moment in his young life, that he gets to sleep with this woman he's obsessed with, and afterwards they show him running down the street to Hall and Oates's "You Make My Dreams Come True."

And all of a sudden everybody on the street starts helping him celebrate that he slept with this girl, and it's this huge thing, and it's a very funny, cute bit of how a guy feels when he's young and he gets a girl that he really wants for the first time. I was watching it with a friend, I think it was Schiff (Mark), and I leaned over to him and I said, "That's how I felt when I passed the audition at The Comic Strip." I said, "I never felt that way when I got a girl. But that day, that was a dream come true. You know, 'cause then I knew that I was on my way."

And you know a funny thing that was a big deal to me, and that I used to tell people? I was performing in a lot of these little clubs—they were kind of low-grade places—but when I passed the audition here at The Strip, if I remember correctly, you had a five dollar cover charge here right?

Well I was very proud of that five-dollar cover charge, that people actually had to spend five dollars to come and see me. I thought that was something really special and a real different level of the business. That five-dollar cover charge made it seem like it was something of value, and it meant a lot to me.

You know, I even remember where I parked that day I auditioned. I drove in from Massapequa, and I parked right near the avenue, on 82nd Street. I was just one block north, and I remember I was on the north side of the street, and I remember everything about it. As a matter of fact, I think that was the last time anyone ever found a spot around here.

But it was certainly the last time I ever auditioned as a comedian for anything. Once you became established here, you were golden. You could go anywhere.

The club was new, I was new, Larry Miller was new. And so we said, "This'll be our place." Frankly, we never felt that comfortable at the other places, 'cause established people really don't want new people coming and taking their spots. The other comedians aren't happy to see you. Especially if you got somethin'.

So we came here and we were able to make this club, and the club in turn made us, and it was a great thing for all of us. They were happy to have us, we were happy to have them, and we were one big, happy family. It was our home, and it was great.

So, after I passed at The Strip, I left Massapequa and moved into Manhattan that September. I was going back and forth up till that point, and my parents couldn't really understand what I was doing. My mother couldn't believe I would be taking a shower at midnight and getting ready to go out. She was like, "What are you doing?" And I'd be like, "I'm going to the club. I gotta hang out at the club and try to get on late."

And she finally said, "Why don't you just get an apartment in the city? Wouldn't that be easier?" And so I did, and I'm still living on the same block thirty-four years later. Isn't that amazing?

I also have the same friends, too. Larry Miller I met on the crosstown bus on our way over to The Comic Strip. He was a bartender and a drummer, and he was trying to get onstage and I was the first act he ever saw when he came in here. So he came over to me on the bus one night and introduced himself, and we've been friends ever since.

And George Wallace I knew from The Strip, too. Anybody who was serious about it was here seven nights a week. You had to hang out with the other comics, and very quickly it became a home.

This club really took care of us. We even ate here. They even gave us clothing. All you really needed was a couple of pairs of jeans, 'cause the club gave us the T-shirts, and maybe you needed a decent shirt for the weekend, and you were golden.

You've been quoted as saying the ultimate goal was getting the nine p.m. spot on Saturday night at The Comic Strip. Do you remember getting your first weekend spot?

First of all, if I didn't actually say that quote, I certainly thought it. And I remember that first weekend spot so well. It's another thing that's crystal clear. I don't remember who actually gave me the spot, because in those days the MC used to make up the lineup.

In any case, I do remember the evening exactly. The audiences in those days here were so excited about these new young comics. They would come in and they were really in a great mood. So I remember going on at nine o'clock in front of two hundred people. It was the biggest audience I had ever faced by far. I had usually performed in front of fifteen or twenty people late night, but this time I went on in front of two hundred people and did my little fifteen-minute act, and it worked really well, and that was it.

I just knew that I was gonna be okay, and I was gonna be doing this the rest of my life. And I remember sittin' at the podium for the rest of the night, 'cause I just didn't wanna leave. I was just enjoying the glow that I had experienced. In my mind, I had made it. I was on my way. I could stand in front of two hundred people and do okay. It was a big deal.

Do you remember any of your early material?

Sure. The first joke I had that was a really big laugh was about the tramway to Roosevelt Island, which had just been built. This was 1976, and I said, "Well, this is great. The city's going bankrupt, and they're putting in rides for us. The next thing I guess we'll have some sort of roller coaster through the ghetto, and that'll be the first roller coaster where they scream on the *flat* part of the ride!" And that was a big laugh.

In those days I wrote material every day, and I still do. To me, that's what being a comedian is. It's kind of working that part of your mind offstage as well as onstage. You gotta be always using your mind. They're paying to hear what you think, so you have to spend part of your day thinking!

I keep a pad with me to write things down. That's my business partner, and it's the only partner I have.

So, in the early days, I hung out here with Larry and George and Mark Schiff and Jimmy Brogan, Mike Cain and Carol Liefer.

Can you tell us about the New Year's brunch and how that got started?

We argue about that. I think it got started on New Year's Day of 1978. A lot of those gigs on New Year's Eve were rough. The people would get drunk. They were tough crowds. They had noisemakers and all and weren't exactly always paying attention, so we wanted something to look forward to. Knowing what we had to endure, we figured we could all get together the next morning, have brunch, and could kind of commiserate on how horrible the night before was, and that's how we started getting together on New Year's Day.[2]

So what made you make the move to LA?

I was performing here at The Strip for about four years, until I went out to LA in March of 1980. I had gotten to be pretty good here and was one of the regular, steady weekend guys, and I could get on at the other clubs, and I just thought, "Well, if I'm getting to the top here, I better be a small fish someplace else."

I didn't really wanna be a big fish here. And everybody always talked about LA. I had never really been there, and I thought, "Well, let's see." You have to keep moving forward.

When I started, I thought to myself, "Oh, I'll be doing this a couple of weeks, and I'll be on *The Tonight Show*." It's so funny; you're so impatient when you're a kid. You don't even know what it is when you start.

Once I decided to move to LA, I told George Wallace that I was gonna give up the apartment, and he said, "Don't give up the apartment, that's a great place to stay when we come back to New York." He says, "Why don't we split it?" So we did. It was $210 a month, and we split that in half.

So when did you get Seinfeld*? (It felt strange asking him that, as if his last name wasn't Seinfeld.)*

That didn't happen until late fall of '88. I had been booked on the Rodney Dangerfield special, and George Shapiro, who was managing me after having seen me at The Comedy Store in LA, wrote to Brandon Tartikoff at NBC, to invite him to the taping of that show here in New York.

---

[2] Paul Reiser remembers this story very differently and tells his own account during his interview.

George had first seen me perform that summer I got to LA, back in 1980, and he wrote a letter to Brandon Tartikoff, which I think is in the National Archives now, and there was one sentence that stuck out in everyone's mind. He said, "Call me a crazy guy, but I think Jerry Seinfeld is someday gonna be doing a TV series on NBC."[3]

And then he just gave him the information if he wanted to come see me at the Rodney thing. I don't think he actually came, but then they called me in to NBC and said, "What kind of show did you have in mind?" And I said I didn't really have anything in mind. And then I was telling Larry David the story at Catch one night, and then we started talkin' about it, and that's how the whole thing evolved.

Now Larry David was a stand-up in those days too. He didn't do The Strip as much as we did. I knew him mostly from Catch. He'd do a set here at The Strip and then he'd go over there and hang out and try and get on again. And that was our swing. It was really great that they were right nearby. You'd just go back and forth all night. Then, we'd all go to The Green Kitchen (a twenty-four-hour diner), which is also still there amazingly, and eat, drink, and laugh all night.

Tell me about Richie Tienken.

Richie was here a lot when I was here. If you didn't see Richie, it was like you felt like you didn't see everybody. That's what was great about the club. You come in, you expect to see the people that you know and like, and you hang out. I guess we were working, and it was our career, but it didn't feel like it. It really just felt like that silly song that they had at the beginning of *Cheers,* that this was your home.

And when we would have gigs at other places, we wouldn't go home afterward; we would come here.

---

[3] George Shapiro confirmed this and told me the exact same "crazy guy" story!

Was Richie intimidating? A lot of comics described him that way.

Well, don't forget, I met him at the very beginning. He wasn't an icon yet, so he didn't have time to become intimidating. He was always very friendly and had a nice way about him. He was in control of the club, and there was no doubt that he was the boss, but you always felt like he had a paternal or a nurturing kind of feeling. Like he was taking care of us.

It was really very nice, and I think that was one of the reasons the club had such a nice atmosphere. These other places, there was a lot of drugs, there was a lot of mischief and mayhem going on thereandabouts, and this club didn't have that.

And I think that's why Larry and I, who were from Long Island—we were suburban kids, we were used to nice neighborhoods—we felt more comfortable here. It was a *haimishe* place.

And what about Bob Wachs?

I met him at the same time. We kind of thought of Bob as kind of a real powerbroker in the upper echelons of show business. We had no idea what he was up to. We knew he was making very important phone calls in a beautiful office somewhere. He was definitely not down here in the swamp with us! He was moving big pieces around.

Those were pretty glorious days. We were usually busy playing ball in Central Park, Hecksher Field, because we didn't have jobs. And there were all those buildings around you, and all those people were up there working under the fluorescent lights, and they got bosses, and they gotta be there at a certain time, and they can't leave, and we were wearing sneakers and T-shirts, playing ball in Central Park, and we just felt like we had it licked.

Did you ever have a day job?

No, never. I never had a day job. Well actually, to be perfectly honest, the story is, I auditioned at The Strip that first summer, and I worked as a waiter during lunch hour at Brew Burger on 3rd Avenue and 47th Street. And I had that job, but the guys at The Strip very quickly gave me the job of MCing Monday nights.

That was the first night that Richie gave me here. And that was like twenty-five dollars. And then somehow I got Friday night, which I think used to be Greg Monahan's night, but those were long nights and I think he had other things to do.

And then when I got my third night, which I think was Sunday night, I think by then I had Friday, Sunday, and Monday, and once I got that third night, which got me to like seventy-five or eighty dollars a week, then I was able to turn in my apron. And that was only four months into it.

Wallace moved out to LA that January. I drove out there with him in his Lincoln Continental, with the seats that didn't recline. The color was called Rose Diamond. And I remember we were driving and I was trying to think of ways to make a little cash, just to get by, and he told me why don't I sell those cup holders that hang in the door, in front of the Midtown Tunnel. That was what he wanted me to do. Sell cup holders.

He said you could buy them for about fourteen cents and sell them for like a dollar or something. And then when I got back to New York, and I got that extra night, that third night, I didn't have to consider that anymore. Not only was the money great, but the stage time was also very, very important. I'll never forget that. That was a very big day in my career when I turned in that apron, 'cause that's when I knew that I would never work a straight job ever again.

I had moved into the city that summer, so it was by the winter of '76 that I finally got my third night. Thinking back about it, I was moving pretty fast for a young guy. I came in here with nothing, and five months later I was MCing three nights a week and had an apartment on West 81st Street.

Do you remember a meeting at The Strip of the club owners to decide whether the comedians should be paid?

Yes, I do. And I know that Richie remembers that also. I remember that they had this big thing in LA that the comedians should get paid, and I thought we should do it here, and we had a meeting here one day, and all the comics came over here. I'm sure it was no different from any union meeting or any of these kinds of things. It was our first introduction to any kind of politics.

People were on different sides of the issue. There were comedians that thought we didn't deserve any money, because we were here to learn, and then there were comedians who thought we did deserve to get paid because we're providing a service and people were paying for it. It was a messy, complicated thing that upset a lot of people at the time.

It had been a very smooth-running thing, and unfortunately the club owners were not smart enough to realize, "Let's give these guys a little bit of money and make this whole thing go away, and everyone could go their happy way." There was a little bit of tension and push-pull that occurred there.

[Author's Note: At this point, Richie interjected: I remember standing with Rick Newman at the bar talking about this thing, and Rick said to me, "I ain't never paid anybody, and I'm not gonna start now." And I said, "Hey Rick, I think we gotta do something."

And then Jerry came walkin' over and said, "Well, I think that the acts should get paid." And Rick said, "Oh yeah, who are you?" And he said, "I'm Jerry Seinfeld. I work at your club." And Rick said, "Oh yeah, we'll see about that."

So Jerry walked away, and I told Rick that Jerry was a good kid and didn't mean anything by it. I basically told him to forget about it.

So anyway, Jerry was all worried about going over to Catch that night cause he had a spot there, and I said to him, "Just go. Rick probably won't even remember. Just go." And he did, and everything was fine.

I encouraged the acts to go to Catch to work, 'cause I wanted them to get better. If they went to Catch to get more stage time, that was fine with me. Then they'd come back here. I wanted a big star to come out of this club. So Jerry was all happy. Not only did he go back to Catch, but he had a good set.]

Can you tell me a couple of funny stories about the old days at The Strip?

Well, there was one thing we used to do that was a little tradition on April Fool's Day. In those days, everybody watched everybody else's act every night. So everybody knew everybody else's act word for word. So Larry Miller and I cooked up this thing where on April 1 for April Fool's, we would each switch acts with somebody else. We would each do somebody else's act, and it was the worst show you ever saw in your life.

Because you can't really do somebody else's act, but we tried anyway, and it was a lot of laughs. And then remember those Christmas parties? We always had the best Christmas parties.

Larry Miller told me that you would show up with at least three new ideas every day written on a little piece of paper, and you would develop them here onstage. And that you were an inspiration to the other guys.

Well, I saw comics get on TV, go on *The Tonight Show*, they'd go on once and do great—first shot's always great—'cause you do all your best stuff, and the second shot it would go down a little, and it would continue to go down, and the next thing you know, six months later, the guy's off the show. A year later, he's done. And I thought, "This is a long career; you can't let that happen."

So I saw early on that you have to figure out a way that you're comin' up with new material all the time.

Is there anything else you can think of to say about The Comic Strip?

I just feel very lucky that it started when I started, and we all kind of came up together. We were very fortunate to all kind of meet at the same place at the same time. It started off my whole career and a lot of careers. But you never forget where you started, and I'm sure without this place it would have taken me many years longer to get known. But because I was able to get onstage, and they made me an MC, I was on a fast track because of this club, and I was able to get somewhere.

Do you believe in coincidence, or do you think things are structured where The Universe has things happen in a way where your life follows an orderly direction? They say that "Coincidence is God's way of remaining anonymous."

I like that saying, and yes, I think I do believe that there is some order to The Universe. That makes sense to me.

Hey, this is my life! When I die, I'm gonna be thinkin' about when I was here. In a way, you know, 1976 to me is the year I was born. It's when I figured out who I was and what I was supposed to be doing, and I figured it out here, so it's all great.

Paul Reiser

Paul Reiser is an actor, comedian, TV personality, author, screenwriter, and musician who got his big break playing Modell in the 1982 Barry Levinson movie *Diner*. He appeared in several films such as *Aliens* and *Beverly Hills Cop 1* and *2*, and his two best-known sitcoms were *My Two Dads* and *Mad About You.*

What year did you start performing comedy, and what are your earliest memories of The Comic Strip?

14

The first time I ever performed comedy was between freshman and sophomore year of college, so that would be the summer of '74, and I did five minutes up at Catch. It was an audition night, and I remember getting there about one in the afternoon to go on about two-thirty in the morning.

So I did five minutes and went back to college, which was SUNY Binghamton, where I was studying music. I was a piano player and composer, I didn't know what I was gonna do, and I was studying business 'cause I thought I was gonna be in my dad's business, a health food wholesaling business. And somebody asked me what I did that summer, and I said I was a comedian.

I liked saying that. Five minutes out of three months, but I labeled myself a comedian. So then sophomore year I did it twice, in 1975, and I don't think I got to The Strip until I graduated in 1977.

But how did you think of doing comedy at all?

I'll tell you exactly. I was never smart enough to figure out a path, and I'm still not. But I always loved comedy. In high school they had this program, a couple of days before spring break, where they had these minicourses where students would teach. You pick a subject you like, and you could organize the thing and teach the class for a couple of days. So me and my best friend Billy Grundfest, who later went on to run The Comedy Cellar, would teach comedy. We'd get records by Mel Brooks, George Carlin, Richard Pryor, and we'd talk about it and try to make it academic, but I used to think to myself, "How do you become a comedian?"

Then in 1973, when Catch opens, you start hearing about Freddie Prinze, Gabe Kaplan, and Jimmy Walker, and it became clear to me that if you go to this place, and you get on line, and you wait for a long time to get on, they give you a sitcom. It looked that way with Freddie. Last year, he was doing nothing, and all of a sudden he had this big TV show.

15

So when I finished college in 1977, that summer I came to The Strip, and me, Carol Leifer, and Rich Hall all auditioned together, and Lucien passed us all the same night. I was living with my parents out in New Jersey but hanging out during '77 and '78, and my father said, "Look, do your bullshit for about a year, then you'll get it out of your system and you'll come to work."

So I kept stretching it out, and now it's December of '79, and he says, "Time's up." And then he sent me to Tulsa, Oklahoma, where he had a subsidiary of his company. He wanted me to learn the business out of his shadow, and I was there maybe six or eight weeks, and that was where I had my moment of clarity.

I would call the comedy clubs back in New York just to hear the background and what was going on. I wanted to hear who was there, 'cause I knew some of the guys. I'd call Pips out in Brooklyn to see who was playing tonight, and somewhere along the line I said to myself, "I don't want to work in my dad's business. I want to do comedy."

And I remember calling Bob Wachs and told him I wanted him and Richie to think about me as a comic and to tell Richie I was serious about performing and that I was coming back, and he advised me to calm down and take it easy.

And when I told my father about my decision—that was a tough afternoon. Ultimately he took it well, but that day was tough. But the way I explained it to him was important. He was saying things like, "How do you know you'll ever get good at it and make any money?"

He was a businessman, and he had started his own business from scratch forty years before, and turned it into a big thing. So I said to him, "I wanna do what *you* did. I wanna start from scratch, and through my own efforts and abilities, I wanna build something. I'm not looking to be a star as of tomorrow. I wanna build slowly and get good." And that, he finally understood.

So in 1979, I moved into New York and got my first apartment in the city on 76th Street, between 1st and 2nd Avenues and The Comic Strip became my home. It was a little studio apartment, $390 a month, and eleven square feet facing a brick wall, and then I started working on my comedy all the time.

In the beginning, I used some savings, but within the year, I was making enough money to support myself. Seventy bucks here, a hundred there, thirty bucks here, enough to piece it together. My rent was $390, and I was eating at The Strip. Life was good.

This club always treated everybody better, and they nurtured you, like Richie giving you thoughts, and Lucien giving you comments, and even Bob Wachs was helpful. And I had been hoping I'd hate comedy so it would have made my life simple, and it would have been easy to go into my dad's business. But whether I had a good night or a bad night onstage, I still couldn't wait to get back onstage the next night.

I remember in the beginning, when I was living in my parents' house in Jersey, I would call up looking for a spot, and the other comics used to tell me I had to hang out. Even Seinfeld used to tell me that, and I didn't understand it. I was like, "I'm working in an office from eight-thirty in the morning until six. I don't wanna start hanging out in some club just to bullshit with everybody."

And Seinfeld described it as being just one of these intangibles. You become part of the community, and sure enough that was exactly right, 'cause if you were part of the community and if someone had a gig and couldn't make it, they'd offer it to you.

With very few exceptions, everybody was supportive. We would even help each other fix their lines.

That's how Jerry became known as "the doctor of comedy," 'cause he'd help everybody fix their lines.

That's right. Jerry was a year ahead of us. When I got here, Jerry was already the MC, and come to think of it, it might have been Jerry who passed me, Carol, and Rich Hall, and not Lucien. 'Cause in those days, the MC booked the show.

I certainly can't imagine that I was really funny when I got here. It's also so hard to remember when you've seen so many comics. It's been so watered down. But it was still kind of new then. Of course there was Robert Klein and David Brenner, David Steinberg, and George Carlin, and Pryor . . . the greats. And even David Sayh, who was MCing at Catch. I saw him at Catch, and I didn't think he was that funny. Then about eight months later, during my senior year of college, I turn on *The Tonight Show,* and he was on, and I'm like, "Jeez! He got really funny!"

And that told me the system works, that there's something to be said for going on every night. If you do it a few times in the summer, you're not getting very far. You go on every night, or as we got the chance, two, three, or four times every night, you may not even realize it, but you're gettin' better.

But maybe he went on before he should have, because a break is a break, but then you gotta deliver. Jerry was always great about giving advice like taking your time, 'cause it's gonna be there. And the other comics were always very supportive, and they'd tell you where the gigs were, or go and see this guy. There were lots of comics, but there were also so many jobs.

How did you get your first Tonight Show?

I wound up doing *The Tonight Show* because I was in the movie *Diner* in April of '82, and I wouldn't have gotten it otherwise, because they had seen me and felt I wasn't ready yet. But now with the movie, it was a different story.

This is a great story. It was February of 1981, and I wound up walking into this casting office with my friend Michael Cain, another comic, who was going there to audition for the movie. I was on my way to Macy's to buy underwear and socks, 'cause I was going down to The Comic Strip in Fort Lauderdale,[4] and I wasn't in the mood to do the laundry, so I was just gonna buy new underwear.

So he says, "Well the casting thing is on Thirty-sixth Street, so let's go together." I'm like, "fine." And it's really weird, 'cause I was never a guy who says, "Let's hang out." So in retrospect, it was very surprising that I would even agree to meet somebody to hang out, 'cause I wasn't a hanger. So we go to the casting office and I'm sitting outside while Michael is doing his thing, and he's finished, and the casting director comes out and says to me, "You're next. Where's your picture?" I'm like, "No, I'm not here to audition. I'm just waiting for my friend, and then I have to go buy socks and underwear." And she says, "Well, do you have a picture?" And I'm like, "I do, but it's at home, and I don't wanna step on Michael's parade here." She says, "Come back tomorrow with a picture." And then we went to Macy's and I bought socks and underwear.

Next day, I come back with the picture, and then I go down to Fort Lauderdale. I'm down there two days when I get the call: "You got the job. To be the sixth guy. The movie's about five guys, and there's gonna be a sixth guy, and his name is Modell, and we're not sure yet what he's gonna do, but you'll flesh him out when you get there."

And I remember talking to the producer in the afternoon at the bar of The Comic Strip, and he says to me, "Do you have any other commitments? Are you free to do this thing?" I remember thinking, "Yeah, I have one Jerry Stanley gig for seventy-five bucks. I bet I can get out of that." So they sent me an envelope from MGM to The Comic Strip address, and I was like, "Wow, this is the real thing. A contract and all."

---

[4] The Comic Strip in Fort Lauderdale, Florida, was short-lived, as compared to The Comic Strip in New York. It opened around 1979, and Richie sold it around 1990.

And it was standard, you know, the lowest thing they could get away with, and Bob [Wachs] was a lawyer, so he said he'd look at the contract, and Richie reads the script from cover to cover, and he says to me, "Did you say your character's name was Modell?" I'm like, "Yeah." He says, "Well I don't know how to break this to you buddy, but you ain't in here. They told you you gotta flesh it out? Well I sure hope so, 'cause you don't have any lines!"

So ironically, I get to Baltimore a month later, like the end of March, and I still had no lines, but Barry Levenson would just let us improvise.

And we'd be sitting down for a meal, and I was the guy who didn't know if I should be sitting with the cast or the extras, 'cause my character didn't appear anywhere in the script. So once in a while they'd say, "Where's Reiser?" and they'd say, "He's with the extras," and they'd say, "Schmuck, you're with the cast." And I was like, "Oh, 'cause I don't have any lines. I don't know whether that counts as cast or not."

Do you remember how you met Jerry Seinfeld?

Yeah, well he was the MC, and he was the guy who was always great. And more than his material, it was his confidence and his discipline. He would come in every night, and he'd open up a little piece of paper with three words on it, and he'd always have three new premises, and by the end of the week, each premise would be a nice joke. And he was always very neat, and it was literally like having a big brother, 'cause he was always a year ahead of you, so he'd tell you about a gig, and a year later you'd be doing it too.

And how did your friendship come to pass? A lot of guys worked together, but not all of them got so close.

I do remember how that happened. At first he was just another guy, and we were acquaintances. Plus he was very helpful, and we all shared a great love for comedy. We also all liked old jokes. So I remember me, Jerry, and Larry Miller would sit at the bar telling jokes, and I would bring in like a great Myron Cohen joke, and sometimes I would even do them onstage. And that may have actually gone on way too long, because I'd say, "Folks, this is not my act, but I gotta tell you this joke." Like the guy who peed in the saxophone joke, or the French toast joke. And you say it's not your act, but after twenty minutes of doing jokes, suddenly you're becoming a jokester.

So it was just the camaraderie of hanging out and enjoying each other's comedy. And because this was still '77 or '78, I was still living out in New Jersey, and I was basically feeling very out of it. I really wasn't feeling much camaraderie in general, 'cause I wasn't hanging out as much, mainly because I had to go home and get ready to go to work in the morning.

But later, I was dating Carol [Leifer]. Carol had gone to college with me, and we did a play together. It was *You Can't Take It With You* by Kaufman and Hart. She was very funny, and I told her she should do stand-up, which she did.

Anyway, we get to The Comic Strip, and I don't really know Jerry too well, but suddenly somewhere along the way I started noticing, "Gee, Carol and Jerry seem to be getting awfully close. What the heck is that?" And then she was kind of hanging out with Jerry, so that was kind of bad. Then it was really awkward.

I didn't really know Jerry, but I was thinking, "Well, he's got the club, and he's working, and he's got my girlfriend now . . . he's doing good!"

But that incident is what led to the famous New Year's brunch that's been going on for the last twenty-eight or twenty-nine years. I can't believe I'm just putting this all together now as we speak. I remember after moving into the city in May of '79, that December we had a New Year's Eve show here at The Strip. And me and Jerry looked at each other and I just said, "Can we get this Carol shit out of the way, 'cause we should be friends, right?" And he said, "yeah," and we shook hands, and I thought, "Wow, this is great! What a nice guy." And he became another comedy brother.

So every year when Jerry, Mark Schiff, Larry Miller, and I have our annual brunch we always wonder, "When did this start?" Now, I know for a fact that it must have started on January 1, 1980, because the next day, after we shook hands, we all went out to Grass, a place on 77th and 1st, or something. We all woke up late and nobody had anything else to do, and I just realized now that it was that handshake that started it!

But what I also remember, and wow, I haven't thought about this either for so long, was the importance of hanging out in the club. It was like having your nose pressed against the window watching all the other people having fun, and I had to go back home to New Jersey, working in the Jersey job, and again I realized what you had to do to be part of this thing.

Making that commitment to come in here was sort of the defining moment of my life. And that was really the last big decision I ever made.

Tell me about Lucien.

Lucien was always a warm and helpful guy to me. He was a little bit of a character 'cause he could get very full of himself and enjoy his own opinion, so he'd go off on a bit and he'd go, "And I'll tell you another thing." And I'd go, "Well, I don't need that much information."

He was very protective also. But again, I started performing here in '79, and I got *Diner* in '82, so in comedy years it was not that long before I had a nice success. It wasn't like I made it or anything like that, but from that time on Lucien was always very hospitable and gracious to me.

Tell me about Richie. What were your impressions of Richie?

In the beginning I saw mostly Lucien, but afterward it was the three dark horsemen. John was the afternoon guy, with the little cooler with the nips. You know, those little beers, six-ounce Schaeffers. And then he'd say something like, "I think I'm gonna drive home now. Just give me six of them for the road." And I'd say, "Is that good?" It's not like he had one. He was taking them to drink in the car. It seemed troublesome. I used to wait till he got home before I got in my car.

Richie was the cool guy. I saw Adam Sandler a couple of weeks ago, and he was doing a great impression of Richie hitting a golf ball down 2nd Avenue, as he did one night. And Adam was going, "Richie, maybe you shouldn't." And then Richie went, "No, no, no, don't worry. It'll be fine," just before the cops pulled up.

Larry Miller

Larry Miller is one of Hollywood's most recognizable faces, having appeared in more than one hundred films and TV shows, beginning with *Pretty Woman* and including *The Princess Diaries* and his starring role in *Ten Things I Hate About You*. He has a podcast, "This Week with Larry Miller," and is a weekly guest on *The Adam Carolla Show*. He is currently touring with his one-man show, *Cocktails with Larry Miller: Little League, Adultery, and Other Bad Ideas*.

What year did you start performing, and what are your earliest memories of The Comic Strip?

Well, I was working at Amtrak. I was about a year or two out of college and thinking somehow I'd like to be an actor or a comic or a writer, something in show business. And someone at Amtrak where I was working said that her cousin, a guy named Tony D'Andrea, was working as a comic and a bartender at a place that just opened called The Comic Strip.

So I went there. I think it was the fall of '77 on a Tuesday night. Tony was bartending, and it was about twelve-thirty or one in the morning. I introduced myself and told him I was thinking of becoming a comic. He just took me back into the showroom and sat me down in the alcove where the comics and industry people hang out and said, "Go ahead and watch the show a little bit." And the first guy I saw go on was Jerry Seinfeld.

I'll never forget it. And Jerry had his Comic Strip T-shirt on, and the MC, Larry Cobb, even mentioned it. "And our next act coming to the stage, wearing his official Comic Strip T-shirt . . ." It was very important to us, having that T-shirt. It was an identity.

We spent seven days a week at that club, and there was no other way we wanted to live. What a way to learn about comedy. I'd watch the shows from eight o'clock until I got onstage, which was like two, three, or four in the morning.

I was living on the West Side on 78th and Amsterdam at a time when the West Side still had a lot of actors and comics and writers because it was inexpensive. In those days, Lucien was there, but I auditioned for someone else. It could have been Richie or Bob. It could have even been one of the MCs, which was at that time the height of what you wanted to achieve. There were three regular MCs then: Larry Cobb, Greg Monahan, and Bob Kinney, and maybe it was one of them who passed me.

Our little crew was a pretty good group of comics. There was Jerry, Paul Reiser, Jimmy Brogan, Carol Leifer, Mark Schiff, me, and a guy named Michael Cain who left us way too young.

At that time the cooler, more established clubs were Catch and The Improv. But we were all at The Comic Strip! And you know what?

We had a lot of great comics that came out of that club that went on to have really great careers!

And, to this day, there is still only one club out of those three that is still going strong and putting on great shows and drawing terrific audiences, and that's The Comic Strip. The others have all gone.

When you got onstage, the introduction you wanted was, "He works all the major showcase clubs in town." That meant you were a good act, a bankable act, and one they would put on at all three clubs. But The Comic Strip was our home club.

Which is why the T-shirts were so important to us. They were a real mark of distinction. They were our varsity jackets.

For a while, I didn't even have a glossy on the club wall. Instead, I used a picture from a Passover seder with my family and I sitting around the table, and you can clearly see that I'm wearing a light-blue dress shirt with a tie, and underneath it you can see a Comic Strip T-shirt, which was not a small thing, considering that I even wore it under my Passover suit!

And when I finally became an MC there, they gave me a Comic Strip jacket. I never took that thing off. I wore it till it evaporated. I was so proud of it. I went up to a school reunion and went to a football game, and I wore my Comic Strip jacket in the stands, and I was really proud of it.

Do you recall the first time you met Richie Tienken?

The first time I met Richie Tienken doesn't stand out in my mind, but I mean that in a good way. It was like he was always there, and in a sense I was always there. Once I started at The Strip, it became such a part of my life. It's like the town you grew up in. I don't really remember a time not knowing Richie Tienken.

Amtrak was a great job, but I knew that eventually I'd have to leave. After about eight or nine months, things had progressed to the point that I was the drummer at The Comic Strip on Friday and Saturday nights, making twenty-five dollars a night. One night, John McGowan came over to me and said, "I know you'd like to devote yourself full time to comedy, so if you want, there's a couple of bartending slots available." The only drag was, I didn't know how to make drinks. I knew how to drink them, but not how to make them.

John didn't want to fire me, so instead he suggested putting me on days, when no customers were there, and I just had to take deliveries and stock the shelves.

The point is, I was drumming two nights a week so that was fifty dollars there, the bartending gig paid twenty-five dollars a shift, so that was another seventy-five dollars a week, and I'm not being flippant now, but I was making $125 a week in cash, and I had more money than anyone's ever had in life, 'cause I was at The Comic Strip seven days a week and seven nights a week, and we'd eat there, we had the T-shirts, we drank for free, and life was perfect.

How soon after you started performing at The Comic Strip did you meet Jerry Seinfeld?

Jerry actually told this story at my wedding. It was on the M17, the cross-town bus, after I passed the audition. We were both going over to The Comic Strip. I was going to hang out, and he was going to do a spot, and I saw him sitting there and went over and introduced myself. I told him I had seen him onstage the other night and that he was great and that I was a comic too. We shook hands and have been friends ever since. At the wedding Jerry said, "He came over and introduced himself to me on the bus, and to this day, I wish I had taken a cab!"

You mentioned music at The Comic Strip. When did they have that?

Friday and Saturday nights, initially we had music. Craig Korman played the comics onstage and then he'd play for the singers too. Then I got to be the drummer, and we had so much fun together. We'd play before the show for the audience and then again later. Guys like Tony D'Andrea and Dennis Wolfberg used music in those days in their acts.

Do you remember your first time onstage at The Strip?

I actually don't. I feel like I was always there. There was no beginning and no end.

Did you write every day?

No, I didn't start writing material until about four years in. Before that, I just went onstage and began to weave words into bits that I would do. At that point, I was proud of that, but that was before I learned about the craft and what maturity is as a performer. It was fine for the time.

I always likened performing comedy to the stages of a rocket. The first stage fires and takes the rocket off the pad. That's the stage of performing, of innocence, of talent, but that's just the first stage.

When that stage burns out, the second stage has to kick in. That's the stage of maturity, craft, technique, about being an adult and wanting to do this well, and putting some thoughts in there. Then that stage falls away too, and the third stage takes over and blends in with wisdom, affection, and all the stages in life that mean anything. That's when I developed what I do now, the legal pad in a hotel room.

Do you remember any of your early material and what you used to talk about?

Sure. One of the first official jokes I ever wrote was how when you go back to high school, you still feel a formal obligation to call your former teachers "mister." You could be the secretary of state, but you'd still call out, "Hey, Mr. Cooper, remember when we set you on fire?" It wasn't a great joke, but it was a good joke.

So when all you guys were hanging out, did you ever help each other with your material?

That was a great part of the fun, and I still do it. When I started getting back into performing again, I'd stick my head into some green room at a club and say, "Listen, how does this setup sound for this or that," just to use as a variable.

Can you remember any interesting connections that came out of you performing at The Comic Strip?

Well, just being there formed me as a comic. It never really mattered to me who was in the audience. Like the other night in Montreal, one of the comics complained that by the time he got onstage, all the network people had left. And I explained to him that it didn't matter. All that matters is that you're a comic, you went up, and you were funny. That's it. They'll see you when they're supposed to see you. That may sound a little "New-Agey" but it's true. Just write jokes and tell them. That's it. That's your job.

Tell me about Richie Tienken.

I think everyone there adored Richie from the day we came in. He always had that aura of someone you could come to. He was very clearly "the believer." And you know, if we were twenty-three or twenty-four, he was maybe thirty-one. He was still a kid himself, but he had a real aura about him, the way anyone does who's the coach of a football team or the CEO of a company. Richie was always very cool, and you just wanted Richie to like you.

And he was always charming and funny. And all the waitresses felt the same way. They were just kind of agog over Richie. I always liked him and I still do. I hope he knows that.

George Wallace

George Wallace spent the first few years of his career in New York perfecting his craft and rooming with Jerry Seinfeld. George was voted number 93 on Comedy Central's list of the 100 Greatest Stand-Ups of All Time. He also has the highest rated 10 p.m. show on the Las Vegas strip.

Can you tell me some of your earliest memories of The Comic Strip?

Back then, George Henry Wallace was a little advertising exec, looking for business, doing cold calls, walking 2nd Avenue, and I see a place called The Comic Strip. I was selling bus advertising at the time. So I said, "Let me walk in here, these people need exposure."

I hadn't seen the room yet, but when I went in, it just so happened that all the owners were there. I met Richie Tienken, Bob Wachs, and John McGowan. I told them who I was and that I wanted to put their business in the street and get them known all over New York City. That was a Thursday evening, and they bought the program, and when we finished the transaction, I told them I did a little comedy act myself.

In those days, I had just started out, and I would come up onstage as a minister, the Reverend George Wallace. I had a robe, the yellow pages as a Bible, and a Jewish Star of David, and I had it all together. I just got up onstage and told jokes. And you know when you're starting out, you don't know all the rules of comedy, and I just told what I thought were real jokes at the time.

I did all kinds of crazy, stupid stuff. Anyway, I sold them that advertising that night, and they said, "You come back tomorrow night and you can audition."

So it's Friday night, I show up, and the place is packed. They put me onstage, and I do my little bullshit act, and they laughed, and I've been onstage ever since.

I had wanted to be a comedian since I was six years old, but I had to grow into it. My plan was to do whatever I had to do to become a successful comedian. So I read the *New York Times* and the biggest money-paying job was in sales, and advertising was always at the top. So I said, "I'm gonna go into advertising sales and make a lot of money," and I did.

I thought I'd lose a lot of money when I finally left advertising, but The Comic Strip paid me back by putting me onstage and letting me be a comedian.

I was so excited to be there, I would help them seat people. I would do everything I could, 'cause I wasn't doing anything else anyway. But thank God for Richie Tienken. He would put me on every night, and we all became friends, and of course I was there with Jerry Seinfeld and Larry Miller and Paul Reiser, who probably came along about a year later.

Some of the guys who hung out with us were big shots from other clubs, like Billy Crystal and David Brenner.

The Comic Strip was my main club. During the day, I was working at MetroMedia selling advertising. I'd get to work every day about ten o'clock in the morning. Cold sales. That was my specialty. I would just walk the streets all over Manhattan, Brooklyn, and Queens trying to rustle up some money.

And that's all I do now as a comedian. I still sell. Tonight, when I go onstage, I got to sell my jokes to the audience. I have to sell it every night, and it has to be fresh every night.

That's why New York comedians are sharper than other comedians around the world, because we had a work ethic back in the day. Some of the new kids, I have nothing against them, but some of them just want to do television. If that's their goal, that's okay, but it wasn't like that for us.

When we started it was just work, work, work. And you can still see that ethic in people like Jerry Seinfeld, Jay Leno, and Larry Miller. Jerry still does concerts on the weekend. There's something about us guys who've been around for about thirty years that we just love to work. And we came up in an era where everything was pretty much clean, you know?

We had Rodney Dangerfield, we had David Brenner, we had Johnny Carson, and all of us guys learned how to do TV by watching and learning from them. We didn't have HBO or anything like that, so we had to be clean. We just grew up that way. I came up in the clean era, and I just like working clean. Anybody can use "M-F" as a punch line, but our goal was to make people laugh with clean stuff.

How soon after The Strip opened did you meet Jerry?

I met Jerry about two weeks into it. We actually met at Catch A Rising Star. We were at opposite ends of the bar. I was looking at this little Jewish boy and he was looking at this little black kid, and we became instant friends.

Then we went over to The Comic Strip, and for some reason he felt sick. He had a cold or the flu, and I said, "You come with me." Remember, I was in advertising, I'm a big shot, and making a lot of money, so I said, "You get into the car with me." I took him to the all-night drugstore on 53rd and Madison, and I got him some Nyquil.

Jerry and I have been friends since then. He had the apartment first on 81st Street, that we later went on to share, and even though I moved out to LA about six months later, we stayed best friends till this day.

Comedians lived on the West Side in those days, 'cause that's all we could afford. If you were a comedian and lived on the East Side, that meant you were doing real good. We shared an apartment for thirteen years together, and then our friend Paul Provenza came in when Jerry left, and he and I shared the apartment.

It was just good growing up in New York and being a comedian. We'd get to The Comic Strip around seven o'clock at night and might not leave till four or five o'clock in the morning.

Do you recall any big break that came directly from working at The Comic Strip?

Yeah, I don't remember the name, but somebody offered me to do a private party in their home. That was a big break for me. And they were giving us maybe $200. Are you kidding? That was huge for those days. Also some people saw me at The Strip and asked me to go up to the Nevele Hotel in the Catskills. This was like the number one Jewish hotel in the world, I'm doing comedy less than a year, and they ask me to do a show at the Nevele. Forty-five minutes.

When you're young, you think you know everything. You think, "Man, I got this down," but I was still new. And in this market, these people have heard everything you could ever imagine. Well, let me tell you, I did so badly, I don't think I got one laugh. Forty-five minutes onstage, and not one laugh. It was brutal. It was so bad that I thought I wanted to jump off the Tappan Zee Bridge on my way back to New York.

Here I am, a young kid, only working maybe six months, and all I've ever worked is The Comic Strip. And some idiot hires me to work the Nevele Hotel. I bombed so badly. You don't know how tough it is to bomb, which is why being a comedian is the toughest job in the world.

There must have been 800 or 1,000 people in the audience, and not one laugh. You can't imagine how that feels.

I was so hurt I couldn't tell anybody. I just told Jerry I didn't do so well. The next night, I went to The Comic Strip and got back on the horse, and people were laughing again. That's why comedy is so good. Yeah, I was down, but I'm back up now. I had wanted to be a comedian since I was six years old, and I wasn't gonna let anything stand in my way.

Then, when I moved to California, within a year and a half I did *The Tonight Show with Johnny Carson.* I did well, and I been doin' good since then.

About two years later, I went back to the Nevele. And there was this waitress—she must have been about seventy years old—she tapped me on the shoulder after the show and said, "Much better this time, eh?" I couldn't believe she remembered. That's how badly I did the first time. Two years later, and she still remembered.

And all of that came out of The Comic Strip. You would go in there every night, and they would support you. It was a real family. The fraternity of the comedians and the owners was a very rare experience.

Tell me about Richie Tienken.

All I know from Richie Tienken is niceness. When we started we didn't know anything, and Richie didn't know too much either about the business. He just came along at the right time, and all of a sudden comedy got hot in New York, and I'm telling you there were lines around the block. And Richie would always take care of us. The first World Series I ever went to was with Richie Tienken. He took me and Jerry to see the New York Yankees and the Cincinatti Reds at Yankee Stadium.

So you and Jerry were really inseparable.

That's what they say, and he is still today my best friend in the world. He's also the nicest guy in the world. And I tell him all the time, that of all the people I could have met, I was so blessed to have met him. Look at him, the number one TV show in the history of comedy.

Now what made you make the move to California?

That was the time when sitcoms were starting to pop up and Jimmy Walker was so hot. So I went out there just to see what it was like, 'cause everybody was making their move, so I decided to move out there too. Moving to California was like going from comedy college to comedy graduate school.

And Jerry came out about a year and a half later, 'cause he was still new too. I should really have stayed in New York, but I had money; I had a job. I was vice pres of the world's largest outdoor advertising agency. I actually opened a California branch while I was out there. They still laugh about that and talk about it even today: "You were rich when you showed up!"

I had gone out there for two weeks one holiday, but while I was there I drummed up about $200,000 worth of advertising business. I knew I wanted to be a comedian, so I said to the office, "We need to open an office in LA." And they said, "If you could do that much business in two weeks and you want to do it, do it." So I did.

I opened up a little office out of my house, and then I started going up onstage at some of the comedy clubs in Los Angeles, like Mitzi Shore's Comedy Store and Budd Friedman's Improv. I was making money there, and I was also making money in advertising, but the advertising started to cool off a little bit, and they asked me what happened 'cause it had started out so strong.

All I knew was that I was doing more and more comedy, which was my goal, and so I told them, "Whatever you guys want to do is fine with me." So we parted ways, and I felt a little shaky about it, but the exact same night I got asked to write *The Redd Foxx Show*. I became a staff writer, and everything worked out from there.

But no matter what, The Comic Strip is still our club today and always will be.

Ray Romano

Ray Romano is a multi-award-winning comedian, actor, and writer best known for his portrayal of Ray Barone in CBS's hit show *Everybody Loves Raymond*, which ran from 1996 to 2005. He has also appeared in the *Ice Age* films and recently starred in the TNT comedy-drama *Men of a Certain Age*. He often does projects with his close friend, Kevin James.

Ray, what were you doing before you got into comedy?

Well, I was a very bad student. I went to three different high schools and then to Queensborough College for about seven years. And that's truthful. So I was doin' a lot of nothin'. I didn't have much direction. I was working for my friend who owned a futon company here in Manhattan, Arise Futon. He was my best friend from Queens, and he owned a couple of 'em. As a matter of fact, I just saw him yesterday and we played golf, and he needed a guy to do the deliveries, the hard labor, and that was me.

So I was making futon deliveries in Manhattan and trying to figure out what my next move is, and I tried comedy for the first time in '82.

Where was that?

First time ever onstage was The Improv on 44th and 9th. That was my first time ever on any stage doing stand-up.

What made you decide to do stand-up?

Growing up in my neighborhood, in Forest Hills, Queens, we had a clique of about five guys, and we were all pretty creative and pretty funny. You hear this story a lot. I think Eddie Murphy once said that he wasn't even the funny guy in his group. We were all fans of comedy, and there was a church community center, and every Sunday night in the basement there was a teen club, and we would play ping pong, and that's when *Saturday Night Live* had just come out, so the five of us decided to put on our own talent show. We called it a "no talent show," and we called ourselves "No Talent Incorporated." We emulated *SNL*. We created and rehearsed our sketches, and we put on a no talent show for all the kids in the neighborhood.

It was a big hit. We did parodies of the kids in the neighborhood, and we loved it. It was really great. We put on three of 'em about three months apart. The last one got recorded on eight track, which'll give you an idea of how long ago that was. So that's where my comedy bug was kind of born, but I was always a fan of watching stand-up on TV. Bill Cosby, I remember the first comedy album, which I used to listen to with my brother, who I slept with, and my buddy Bill came to my house and played this album for me, and it was all observational family stuff, and he was kind of the guy who got me hooked in stand-up on telling stories like that.

I just related to it so much, and it appealed to me so much. My style is kind of that way. I think he was a big influence on me. And then I used to watch stand-up on TV all the time, and people would tell me I had to try it out, and I remember hearing about audition night at The Improv. So I called up and asked how it worked, and they said the first Sunday of every month, you come down and pick a number out of a hat, and if you pick a number from one to twenty that afternoon, you go on that night. So to increase my odds, I took someone with me.

I even remember who I took. I took a girl who wasn't a girlfriend. She was a girl I knew from the neighborhood, Katie McCarthy, and she came, and of all people she drew the number. Luckily, we had a plan 'cause if you were the person who drew the number, you had to tell them your name, so we had to plan that if she got the number, she would have to use kind of an androgynous name so I could perform that night. So she said, "Jackie Roberts," and I went on that night as Jackie Roberts. Not only that, I passed the audition as Jackie Roberts and had to continue performing under that name for the first two months I was performing. That's the only name Silver Friedman knew me by. And I was afraid to tell her I had lied.

And then I gave it up. I kind of had beginner's luck when I started. On audition night, the audience is so generous and so giving. You do better than you really are. That's what kinda happened to me. I thought this would be kinda easy, but then I experienced bombing and gave it up for about two years. When I came back, I came back to The Comic Strip.

What inspired you to come back?

Well, it was always there. But I came back as Ray Romano. I hadda fake Jackie Roberts' death and make sure everybody forgot about him. And I made Katie sign a confidentiality agreement. But it was always there under the surface, and I kinda felt like I gave up on my dream, and I said, "Let me give it a shot." I was still delivering futons during those two years, and that was definitely not my dream.

I was floundering in school, delivering futons, living at home with my parents, which I did till I was twenty-nine. Twenty-nine years old, living in my mother's house. But you know, an Italian mother doesn't want you to go. She still wants me home *now*!

So you're doing all this stuff for two years, and how did you first hear about The Comic Strip?

It was about 1983. I was driving a truck in the city, so I kind of knew my way around the city and as a wannabe comic, I also kind of knew where all the clubs were. So when it was time to try again, I would just call the clubs and ask about their audition policy, just trying to get the balls to do it again. But I knew that Seinfeld started here, and the club had a great reputation by the time I was ready to make my comeback!

And I continued delivering futons for at least the first two years I was performing again. It wasn't till I knew that I could make a living doing comedy that I knew I could leave the day job. I was already married and living with my wife when I said, "I'm gonna give up the futons and take the leap, and it's stand-up or nothing." And it was nothing for a while!

We did an episode about that on *Raymond* about Claude's Futons, 'cause my buddy's name is Claude who has the futon business, and we used that backstory as the flashback to how I met my wife. In real life I didn't meet my wife that way. In the show, she comes to the door naked, I deliver the futon, I leave, she goes to take a shower, I realize I forgot something, I go back and knock on the door, she runs out of the shower, I walk in, and she's naked, and that actually happened to me delivering futons here in the city.

I even delivered a futon to Larry David. And this was when he was on *Fridays*. Remember, he had been on that show *Fridays* and then it got canceled? So I remember delivering a futon to him, and he complained about it, and we had to go exchange it in his apartment. Typical Larry. I went in, and he was there, and he was talking to me, and I was talking to him, and it's just so bizarre that years later we wound up with our own shows.

I heard that your first paid gig was at The Comic Strip. Is that true?

Yeah, I had been onstage for about three or four months. And I just remembered that the very first time I taped myself performing was here at The Strip. But after only a few months, I really didn't have an act. I had about ten minutes of shaky material, you know? But I was doing my thing. People told me to just go to the clubs that you're allowed to hang out at, and I believe I was passed here by Lucien. Scott Blakeman was MCing a lot in those days, but he didn't have the authority to pass me, so I'm sure it was Lucien. Lucien told me I could come and hang out and do late night when there were still bodies here . . . I don't know that I'd call them actual audiences, but they were bodies, and that I could go up and do spots. Not paying spots, but spots.

So I was splitting my time between here and The Improv, and one night I got here a few minutes early for late night. The last guy on the booked show canceled, and I was the first guy scheduled for late night, so they gave me his spot. I went up and did my time and went back to the bar going over my set: They laughed at that, they didn't laugh at that. And one of the other comics, who I think was Mike Berger, told me, "You know, you get paid for that." And I'm like, "Why?" And he said, "'Cause you took a slot. They owe you money." I didn't have the balls to ask, so he asked the bartender, and the next thing I knew they were handing me seven dollars. My first paid gig. And I gave it all to my wife!

And I also heard that you met your longtime manager Rory Rosegarten here?

I believe I was doing a contest. I think it was the preliminaries for the K-Rock contest. It must have been around 1988, 'cause I had just gotten married. I wouldn't say I was polished, but I was more polished than before. So K-Rock was having a contest and they were giving away ten grand for the funniest new comic in New York, and I had made it to I guess a semi-final, and it was here. I had a great set and that's where he saw me, 'cause he was one of the judges, and he was one of the judges in the finals also. But Brian Regan won the first year, and I won the second year.

Rory saw me the night Regan won, the first year, and that's when Rory signed me. That way he got part of the ten grand I won.

What's amazing is that you guys have stayed together all these years. It's very rare, and it's like twenty-two years already.

Yeah, it's like my marriage. But only one of them fucks me, and it ain't my wife! Rory and I hit it off, and we became friends and that's the important part. It can't only be business. You need a friendship behind it.

Tell me about the Christmas videos that you used to make once a year for the annual holiday party here at The Strip.

It started while I was here. When I became one of the working comics in the city, The Strip was one of the clubs I would play every weekend. I was a regular here, and I had my kids already, the twins and my daughter, so I tried not to do too much time on the road. I'd do like a couple of weeks on the road and then try to make my money in Manhattan so I could stay here. I would do The Strip as much as I could. So when it came time for the Christmas party, they always had a great party and comics would make homemade videos.

So I had an idea about making one about my twins and about how frickin' crazy it was. I think the first one I did was when my twins were first starting to walk and they were very shaky. Me and Danny Kinsella, another comic, were supposedly gambling on who could knock them down with Nerf balls. It was hysterical. First it was I would stand them up, and we would bet on which one would fall first just by themselves. Then we each had Nerf balls, and we each picked a twin and had to try and knock the other guy's twin down first with the Nerf balls.

So we made this for the Comic Strip Christmas party, and I was just as nervous watching that from the back of the room as I was performing, but it was a big hit. And the next year I made one how I would exercise with my twins using them as weights. I just wound up doing one every year. I got a charge out of seeing the crowd enjoy the films. But I ended up using one in my act. When I play Vegas, I still close with the "Silent Night" video I made for the club, interspersing all the crazy things my twins did when they were little, while playing "Silent Night" in the background. I just played Vegas recently, and I still use it to close my show.

But in the days when I first got *Raymond,* I still made the annual films, 'cause it was like a tradition, but eventually, I didn't have the time anymore, 'cause they started paying me a lot of money, and I wasn't able to take the time out to make them.

What was your big break, and how did you get Raymond?

Well, I had become a regular here. I was doing all the clubs, and I did most of the talk shows. I got *Evening at The Improv* and *Rosie O'Donnell*, and this was at the time that comics were getting snapped up for sitcoms. So I had been doing it for like eleven years now, and I was thinking that if it's gonna happen, it should happen around now. And I was kinda getting a little discouraged 'cause it wasn't happening, then the *Letterman* people, with Rob Burnett the producer, watched me do a half hour.

I did it at The Strip, and the club was nice enough to let me do a whole half hour before they agreed to give me a spot on *Letterman*. Lucien let me do it on a Saturday night with a packed house, and I got my *Letterman* spot. When it ended, I thought I had done pretty well, and I thought to myself, "If anyone's thinking of giving me a development deal, if they see that it should happen." And it didn't happen right away.

About a week or two went by, and then Rob Burnett called me at my house on a Saturday and said, "We were thinking of signing you to a development deal, so don't sign with anybody else." And I was honest and I told him, "There's nobody else! I could sign right now."

So Worldwide Pants signed me, and we developed *Everybody Loves Raymond*. The show debuted in '96, so that must have been like '94 or '95. Yes, I did *Letterman* in '94, and we developed the show through '95, and it came on in '96.

And who did you work with to develop the concept for the show?

I went to LA, and they set up like ten meetings with show runners to potentially collaborate with me, and I clicked with this one guy

Phil Rosenthal. Yeah, I had the dysfunctional, neurotic Italian family and he had the same in a Jewish family. It was basically the same. To tell you the truth, there was one other guy I liked—I think his name was Michael Borkow—and it was between those two. He was one of the writers and producers on *Friends*, which was the hot show at the time. Our choice was to go with him, and when we made that choice, he wound up not being available. He took another job with someone else, and we were lucky enough to go with Phil. It's one of those lucky things that has to happen. And nothing against Michael Borkow, but he wasn't a married guy with kids, and this is what the show ended up being about, so I don't think it would have happened that way if we had gone with him.

So it all happened just the way it was supposed to.

I guess so. My wife thought so, 'cause she always thought she was supposed to be rich!

Tell me about Richie Tienken.

Richie Tienken. I was always scared of people with power, and he was definitely one of those guys. I was scared of Silver Friedman too, and I don't know who'd win in a fight between her and Richie! But Richie Tienken was always good to me, and he wasn't around as much then as he is now, 'cause he was with Eddie Murphy in LA. I was kind of under Lucien's tutelage, and I know he kind of spoke well of me, so the times that Richie saw me, I did well, 'cause on any given night you never know how it's gonna go. And whenever he would talk to me, he would encourage me and tell me how great I was doing. I, of course, thought he was lying, because I'm neurotic, but I realized I didn't have anything to be frightened about, which is very true of many things in my life. He was always good to me. He always gave me stage time and encouraging words.

This was a club where you wanted to go to work there. There are lots of clubs where the club owner doesn't really care about their show—they just care about making the money—and this was one of the places where quality really mattered. Richie helped guide a lot of comics. It was definitely a feeling of nurturing and not just caring about the buck.

Someone once said, "The way to make money in comedy is not to worry about making money in comedy." And it was true. Just worry about being good. The money will follow. And that's kind of the vibe you got here. And what was important too was that Richie wasn't a frustrated performer. That makes it tough when the club owner thinks he's funny.

So who were some of your contemporaries? Who did you come up with in those days?

Wayne Federman. Scott Blakeman was always great to me; he was the MC. Joey Vega, J. J. Ramirez, Mike Sweeney, Nick DePaolo, Dave Attell, Brian Regan, Jonathan Solomon, John Manfrelotti, Mitch Fatel, Alan Havey. Havey was a guy who, when I was a late-nighter, I used to think he was the funniest guy I had ever seen. I was always afraid to go on after him.

To sum up, what do you want to say about The Comic Strip?

My feeling is, now that I'm kind of removed, I have to say that it's great just sitting here, because my world has kind of shot off into something I never thought of, and I'm not complaining, but sometimes you miss . . . "I miss the hungry years."

I'm not gonna say I'm not happy now, but I was never more happy than when I was here at The Strip, just learning it all and experiencing the camaraderie of everybody and Lucien telling me about the science of it and me kind of getting what he was saying. It was a real brotherhood here that I kind of miss now. 'Cause look, people are great where I am now, but the bond that I had here is hard to find anywhere in my life now, so it's really great to be here again.

You have such humility despite all of your success.

The truth is, I'm too insecure to be a dick! I try to be a dick, but I just don't have it in me.

Alan Colmes

Alan Colmes started his career as a stand-up comic. He's best known as a radio and TV host, blogger, and political commentator for the Fox News Channel. He spent thirteen years as the cohost of Fox News Channel's *Hannity and Colmes*.

What are your earliest memories of The Comic Strip?

Well, this was around 1976. I was living in New Haven at the time, and I heard this new club was starting called The Comic Strip that would actually give you times to go on. I used to drive in from New Haven to do sets at The Improv and Catch A Rising Star. I was a radio disc jockey at the time.

I was on WABC in those days. I did overnights and then I did the morning show. I was in syndication, starting around 1990, which was when I stopped doing stand-up. It was a very difficult choice for me to make, but I had so many other things going on, I felt I was doing the right thing.

But when I first came over to The Comic Strip, Richie Tienken, the owner, was managing a guy at that time named Buddy Traina, a singer, and Rich gave me Buddy's record to play on the air. We didn't have CDs back then. It was all vinyl. So I thought to myself, "Maybe if I play this guy's record, I can get to perform at The Comic Strip."

At the other two clubs, mostly The Improv, the general rule there was you'd be ignored. I'd hang around all night with the other comics, hoping to get up, and then drive back an hour and a half, get a couple of hours sleep, and then come back in and do the exact same thing again the next day.

And then here comes Richie Tienken, with a brand new club, who always treated the comics with respect.[5]

I'd always drive in because I knew I had a definite place to go up. And another reason I get so emotional about this was because I remember one of the things that made this club different from the others is this club had respect for *all* of the acts. They even had respect for the acts that were not that good, and I was among them.

In the beginning, I didn't really know what I was doing, but they always encouraged me. That made all the difference in the world. And that memory sticks with me, and I guess it always will.

Do you remember who passed you when you came in to audition?

I recall coming in on a Monday night to audition. I think for sure that Lucien was here, but it might have been Bob Wachs who saw me.

I came in with a singer/songwriter named Brian Gari, who was Eddie Cantor's grandson. He used to accompany me on the piano.

---

[5] At this memory of how nice Richie was to him, Alan was so overcome with emotion that he was moved to tears. It just shows how painful it is for young comics, who are really just sensitive artists, to experience harsh treatment and feelings of rejection early in their careers.

I met my manager here, Rory Rosegarten, who's been my manager ever since. He was managing Joe Bolster and Robert Klein, who he still manages to this day. I was his third client, and he went on to represent Ray Romano, Dennis Regan, Brian Regan, and many others. So this was really my home, and obviously to this day, it brings up great emotion in me.

What year did you start performing?

Well, the club opened on June 1 of 1976. I guess I started performing a year or two before that at a place called Al and Dick's. It was a steakhouse that also happened to be a comedy club, and they would serve steaks, and there were people who were there to eat steak and that's all they wanted. They were annoyed to be told jokes while they were eating. They're like, "Leave me alone. I'm here to eat my steak!"

So after that, it was great to have a club like The Comic Strip that gave us a time to go up and put us up to perform for people who were actually there to see comedy.

What was the social life like hanging out at The Strip?

Well, we'd go to The Boatyard on the corner. Then next door, there was Ali's Pizza. And Ali thought he was actually Mohammed Ali. He was a boxer, and if he shook your hand he'd likely break it. If you just looked at him, he'd frighten you to death.

There was a real sense of camaraderie in this club. There was a softball team, but I didn't play because I was a tall, skinny runt.

Christmas parties were great, and we could do jokes about each other and it was taken in great stride, and it was one of the few times we didn't have to pay for the burgers. They would always give us a drink or two.

Who are you in touch with from those early days?

I saw Jerry and Chris Rock at the memorial for Lucien, which was very touching, and it was great that they came.

Through Rory, I see Ray Romano every once in a while, or Joe Bolster. But it's like a brotherhood—or sisterhood. There's gotta be a better word that encompasses both genders . . . maybe personhood. If you've been through this kind of thing and survived the clubs and have paid your dues, it's a brotherhood, or sisterhood, that you never forget.

Tell me about Lucien. What do you remember about him?

Everybody had a loving relationship with Lucien, and Lucien could carry on a conversation with or without somebody on the other end. You might just say "hello" to Lucien, and he might start with, "Well, first the earth cooled," and he could go on for months. You have already left to do a set, or go home and change, or went on vacation, and he would still be talking when you came back.

He was a really great guy. He certainly loved comedy and knew all the acts very well. They would all kid him about being loquacious and speaking a lot, but he was very kind.

Tell me about Richie Tienken.

Richie is and always was a great guy. His love of the business, his love of the acts, his love of the club, the sweat and blood he put into this place basically shows in terms of who the alumni are. And it's also why some of the employees have been here so long. It's not by accident that this club has been here since 1976.

Can you recall any particular break you got out of performing at this club?

I got a lot of things from working here. To this day, I have the same manager, Rory Rosegarten, who I met one night at this club. He used to hang out here all the time. He wasn't interested in me right away, but eventually I wore him down.

I auditioned here for stuff. I did a Woody Allen movie called *Stardust Memories*. I got occasional commercials from being here. I even got one of my first corporate gigs from here. It was for Quaker State, and they flew me to Phoenix and paid me $5,000 just to go and make fun of the corporate bigwigs. And that wasn't too shabby.

You might have only made cab fare here, but what came out of it was tremendous. My career really took off when I got with Rory, who was really focused on comedians and broadcasters and the kind of stuff that I do.

But I always stayed in touch with Richie and never forgot the club, and they obviously never forgot about me either!

Paul Provenza

Paul Provenza is an actor, comedian, writer, and interviewer who directed the hit film *The Aristocrats*. He is also the host and a co-producer of Showtime's *The Green Room*.

The Comic Strip opened in 1976. What are your earliest memories of it?

Actually, my earliest memory of The Comic Strip was from before it opened. When I was in college, I was at the University of Pennsylvania in Philadelphia, but I had already started fooling around with stand-up in high school. I went to the Bronx High School of Science so, from like 1972 to 1975 when I graduated, I used to go to the Improv all the time. I was a patron there before I ever performed there.

I would watch Carlin and Robert Klein and all my heroes, and whenever I saw them on talk shows and they asked where they started, all I would hear was The Improv, The Improv, The Improv.

Now, I had this dream of being a comedian, so I went to the phone book and I looked up The Improv, and I went and started hanging out there and eventually wound up getting on the audition line, but before I did that I would just go and hang out.

I had a couple of friends who were also into it, and we were all under age, but we had fake IDs so we could drink. But it was never like a "go out drinking" night; it was always a "go out and see comedy" night. And I saw Andy Kaufman and Robin Williams before he was famous. Robert Klein used to pop in and work stuff out. Rodney Dangerfield. Joan Rivers used to stop in and do stuff every once in a while. Brenner was already West Coast, but whenever he was in New York he would stop in there.

So after I passed the audition at The Improv, I would drive in from Philly to New York on weekends and holidays.

Bob Saget was at Temple at the same time I was there, and there was no comedy scene in Philadelphia. So myself and a couple of other people would stage little comedy shows in dorm rooms or little clubs in town, and promote them in the dorms. I held auditions for one of those shows and Bob Saget came and auditioned for me. That was back in 1975.

I used to read *Backstage Magazine* 'cause I was also trying to break into acting, and one day there was this little ad about a new comedy club that was opening, and they were looking for performers, comedians, singers, cabaret acts, so I just went, and it was The Comic Strip.

The place was still under construction and hadn't even opened yet. I had just gotten out of high school, so this was in 1975, and it was the summer before I started college. So it was the middle of the afternoon and there were a bunch of guys hangin' out waiting to go on, and I got up for the open audition thing and I had to get up and do ten minutes.

As I recall, Richie and Lucien watched the auditions, and Lucien was really, really very nice to me. He kept saying, "You really have some talent." And I'm like, "Oh yeah, the bartender thinks I'm talented. That's good!"

But Lucien, of course, was a lovely guy, and years later when he was managing the club, whenever I came in he would always make a spot for me. So I didn't actually pass that audition, but I never actually passed the audition at The Improv either. I was just sort of testing the waters. I didn't really have any skill or craft; it was just a dream of mine. All I had was the balls to get up onstage. I was pretty fearless and didn't give a shit about anything. I just wanted to do it so much. I would have suffered anything to be able to perform.

Do you remember any of the material you were doing in those days?

It was just jokey stuff really. Though some of it was about my relation-ship with my father. I do remember one joke, which I'm actually bringing back for a bigger idea that I'm working on now, and it typifies my entire relationship with my father, which was very profound. He died when I was only seventeen, which was right around the time I started doing stand-up.

I was going on all these auditions without even telling anybody, so my parents didn't even know, 'cause I had a very difficult relationship with my father. He probably would have gotten violent about it, because you were supposed to go to college and get a degree and get a regular job or something.

So I guess even then it had the seeds of something personal, but this one joke of any substance was how I would come home with a 99 on a test, and my father would say, "What happened to the other point?" and

I'd say, "Any day now it's gonna be on the end of this heroin needle. Are you happy now, Dad?"

And you know it was really true and honest for a kid of my age. Most of it was just funny ideas or thoughts, no skill or craft, but the only way you'd learn is by doing it.

So I stayed in Philly for college and then on Friday nights I'd drive in the two hours, go to my house in The Bronx, and then go down and hang out at The Improv, trying to get onstage.

But The Comic Strip was always on my mind. They rejected me before they were even open, and nobody knew who they were. I was determined to make my mark there.

Sure enough, one night Lucien remembered me, and he asked me to come in for another open mic night, so I went in and did that and then they said, "Sure, you can work here any time you want." But by that time, I already had a little bit of a reputation of being one of the new young guys who maybe had some potential.

I don't even think Lucien was managing yet at that point, but he already had enough influence to make things happen. Richie and Bob weren't really coming to the open mics anymore.

So I always had this thing that I should be working at The Comic Strip because it was the only place that had ever rejected me, and it was a goal of mine to be accepted there. Every place else, it wasn't an outright rejection. It kind of dragged on like, "Yeah, come back another time, come back another time." But with The Comic Strip, it had been an official rejection. They said, "No, we're not interested." And rightly so.

But that actually gave me the incentive to think, "I'm gonna crack that one."

Because my home base had been The Improv, I didn't get to hang at The Strip as much as Seinfeld or Paul Reiser, Larry Miller, Carol

Leifer, or Rich Shydner. But whenever I had a TV shot coming up or something important, and I really needed stage time, I could always pop in at The Comic Strip and they would put me up.

So it got to the point where I would go to The Improv and because I was new, you either got a very, very early spot or a very, very, very late spot. So I'd go to The Improv and get an early spot, then I'd go uptown and go to Catch and try and get on there, and sometimes I would and sometimes not, and then I'd go to The Strip and go back and forth trying to get on in both places 'cause they were so close to each other.

When did you meet George Wallace and Jerry Seinfeld?

I met George a little bit into the '80s, probably '83 or so. And we became good friends right away. Jerry and I have always been friends, but it's very tough to get real close with Jerry. He doesn't really wear his heart on his sleeve at all. It's hard to get close to him especially if you're not into sports, which is the only other thing you get close to Jerry with. His closest friends are big baseball nuts, and I wasn't into sports at all. So we never got that close, but George and I got very close.

We used to travel together, and we wound up sharing an apartment for many years together, the same apartment he had previously shared with Seinfeld.

Tell me about Richie Tienken.

You wouldn't believe this, especially knowing Richie now, but when I first met him, I thought he was a low-echelon gangster. And all the rumors that went around were that Bob Wachs was this high-powered attorney with a lot of money who wanted to open a nightclub, and Richie Tienken was a mobster who had a liquor license from some bar he owned in The Bronx, and that's how they got together, but they didn't really get along, and Bob Wachs was like this financial wizard and

Richie Tienken was just this thug, which of course turned out not to be true. But there was a really weird thing between him and Bob, and I was never really sure who did what.

Richie was the guy who dealt with all the liquor distributors because supposedly they were all mob connected.

Richie and Bob were just an odd pairing, so nobody knew what to make of it. And in those days, Richie was not always the kind, sweet guy he is now. He would just come out and go, "You suck. You suck. Go learn how to be funny! You suck!"

He was very direct. No beating around the bush. If he didn't like your act, you knew it. And I'm not even saying that in a bad way. I needed and appreciated that kind of honesty. He was a stand-up New York guy with no bullshit.

But he'd also put his arm around you and have a few laughs with you and everything . . . he was a real friendly guy, but he was very direct!

At my stage now, I crave the kind of directness that Richie exhibited in those days. Because his nature was what I grew up with in an Italian family, I also found it affectionate and charming. I knew it, and I wasn't scared of him at all, but I always wondered, "How is he gonna be tonight? Is he gonna tell me I suck tonight, or is he gonna buy me a drink?"

So when did you find out he wasn't a gangster?

I never did, and I'm still not sure!

How was your relationship with Lucien?

I had a lot of interactions with Lucien, all good. If I popped in he would always make sure to give me a spot. But it didn't happen before it should have. I didn't get that kind of respect from him until I deserved it.

He was always a decent human being to me, but he wouldn't just give me spots because he liked me. I had to earn them, and then once I did, I felt like I became one of The Comic Strip family.

Chris Rock

Chris Rock is a comedian, actor, screenwriter, TV and film producer, and director. He was voted the 5th Greatest Stand-Up Comedian of All Time by Comedy Central. He's appeared in films, starting with *Beverly Hills Cop 2*, and recently was up for a Drama League Award for his starring role on Broadway in *The Motherf**ker with the Hat*. He is also the executive producer of a new late-night TV show on FX starring comedian W. Kamau Bell.

So Chris, what year did you start performing comedy, and what are your earliest memories of The Comic Strip?

I started performing comedy in either '84 or '85, but it's more likely that I started in '84 and didn't pass at The Strip until '85. It was one of those things. They were very strict. I remember that Monday night was audition night, and you had to come in early and take a number, and if you were lucky enough, you got to be one of maybe seven or ten people to audition.

And as I recall they didn't even do it every week in those days. It was maybe like one audition night every two weeks, or maybe even once a month, whereas Catch had it every week.

I was conscious of The Comic Strip because Eddie Murphy recorded his first comedy album here, so if you looked at the back of the album you'd see him literally on this stage. I guess that's where I got the inspiration to be a comedian. The guy was bigger than Prince or Michael Jackson. He was huge.

My first memories were like it was a magical place. It was like a comedy factory in a sense, and I know that sounds strange to use that word, but on the one hand it was magical onstage, and then you're offstage and it's very structured. You know, like I knew nothing about show business or anything, so you tend to think it's all like magic. But it wasn't a whole lot different than loading trucks at *The Daily News*, which is what I had been doing.

It was like in that movie *On The Waterfront* and guys stood outside and they put their name on a list waiting to get picked for work. It was the same way for comedians. Some guys were on the list and were regulars, but others of us had to wait. It was weird to get into show business and see how organized and businesslike it was.

It's interesting that you used the word "factory" because Paul Reiser was the only other comic who said the same thing. He said he used it in the best sense of the word, because they churned out good comics one after the other.

Wow, you mean you do this every night . . . and there's a schedule? For somebody who's not in it, it's really a revelation. At least it was for me. So here, they didn't let me onstage early on. The secret of my success is that I don't take no for an answer. I was a teenager. I had no qualms hanging out. As a matter of fact, I had no qualms hanging out all night and not getting on. I *love* stand-up comedy.

So I'd sit back there, in the back of the room, or stand by the wall or find some crevice for myself, 'cause this place was packed on the weekends. But during the week there was more room, and I would literally watch guys from eight-thirty until one-thirty in the morning.

I was from Bed-Stuy, dropped out of school in the tenth grade, and I was just doing shape-up work and bus boy work and stuff like that. I couldn't even tell you what year that was. It's so horrible. I went to school so little it's even hard for me to figure out. Most people graduate from school; they usually know the year. I think I should have been in the class of '85, but I'm really not sure.

I took my GED about six months after I dropped out. I've been a bad student my whole life, literally from kindergarten all the way through. Then one day it just dawns on me: What would be the difference between a GED and my high school diploma? It's not like I'm really gonna use this diploma to get into a college or anything. A GED doesn't even have grades on it.

So you're doing shape-up work. How do you even know you're funny?

I just liked comedy. I just liked it. It was just one of those things. And you don't have to look good. Really, how many parts of show business does it not matter what you look like? You don't have to be physically gifted. And I know when you're young you think otherwise, but stand-up comedy is the only fair part of show business. You make it on your merits and not on your looks.

Stand-up comedy is fucking fair. Not like music. Who's this guy, Timbaland now? You hire Timbaland; you got a hit record. Eddie had a hit record with Rick James. You hire a hit producer you can get a hit record.

But stand-up, you can't fake it. It doesn't matter who you know. You can't fake it. It doesn't matter who your manager or your agent is; it just doesn't fuckin' matter. You really think they wanted to give Roseanne Barr a show? She was just funnier than every pretty girl they tried to give a show to. Rodney Dangerfield? You just go on down the line. Looks have nothing to do with it. It's strictly based on talent.

So anyway, I used to hang out for a long time before I got on. At one point, Lucien had made me a deal that if I stacked chairs at the end of the night that he'd let me get onstage. So sometimes I'd make rounds of the other clubs and come back here late, and me and a nice college kid named Mark Rader would stack the chairs in exchange for stage time. Either he or

I would be the last act, and [Colin] Quinn would even be here sometimes working as a bartender.

So let me get this straight. You come in here as a teenager, and what do you do? Do you pay admission for a show? Do you introduce yourself to people as a comic? What do you do?

Well, like I said, I auditioned and didn't pass, but I just kept hanging out anyway. I just got to hang around a lot. People didn't question me. I was younger than everybody and looked even younger than I actually was. If I had looked older, somebody would have probably said something, but because I looked so young, I had a very Henry Hill existence. And I knew to shut up.

Like now, and I don't mean to sound like a snob, but sometimes I'll come into a club and some kid'll come up to me and say something like he's a friend of mine, "Hey Chris," and whatever else he says, and try to start a conversation. And again, I don't mean to sound like a snob, but when I was coming up, no one would even *dare* think of approaching Rodney Dangerfield. What are you crazy? Are you fuckin' crazy? Only the club owner and maybe a couple of headliners would approach the star. You can't be a fucking kid and approach the star. You can't just fuckin' walk up to Robin Williams or someone like that. You didn't do that in my day. So I knew my place. No one had to tell me that.

I just stayed out of the way. I didn't bother anyone. And if I didn't get stage time, it wasn't that big a blow to me, 'cause I could always see guys who were funnier than me. And if not funnier, at least a better comedian than me. I totally rationalized it in my head: Dennis Wolfberg is funnier than me. Joe Bolster is a better comedian than me. Joe Bolster is *still* a better comedian than me.[6]

---

[6] Jeffrey Gurian's note: Wait till Joe Bolster reads this. To me, it's comparable to the time when Jack Rollins asked me why he never managed me. I didn't know whether to feel good about it or to kill myself.

Do you remember any of your early material?

I talked a lot about race, and Bernie Goetz was news at the time. Jesse Jackson was running for president and Vanessa Williams was the first black Miss America before she got into all that trouble. And with all that, she is probably the most successful Miss America there ever was. There's something rock and roll about her no matter what she's doing. She could be hosting a show like Regis and Kelly and you'd still know she was a bad motherfucker!

What's the real story about the night you met Eddie Murphy?

It was one of those nights I came in, just like I always did, not on the schedule, just to hang out. And I remember a bunch of Porsches and great cars out front, and in those days it was kind of rare to see a Porsche or a Rolls Royce. It was a big deal, so anyway I come in and they say, "Eddie Murphy's here."

So I see Eddie, but again, in those days, you didn't just walk up to famous people. You just didn't do that. Of course I kinda looked, but I didn't say anything. I guess Richie talked to Lucien, and the next thing I knew I was onstage. Richie said that Eddie wanted to see a black comic, and I was the only one around so they put me up. And it was a Friday night, prime time, and the place was packed. I had never been onstage in front of more than like twelve people or whatever, and here the place was filled, and I went on in front of Eddie Murphy, and I did great.

And Eddie liked it, and I knew that because you could hear that distinctive laugh of his all through the room, and I thought to myself, Wow, and we've been friends ever since. Next thing I know, I'm hanging out with Eddie Murphy, going to LA, and it was amazing.

And it was funny because I said I did great, but it was no better than Joe Bolster, Dennis Wolfberg, or Joey Vega. It was my first time before a major audience, so for me it was great. But to put it in perspective, those guys probably did better than me.

So I come offstage and Eddie starts talking to me about the business. It was really weird. One thing about Eddie, he always talked to me like he knew I was going to make it. He was like, "Well, first you'll do this, and then you'll do that." He was giving me advice on buying my mother a house, and I didn't even have any money yet. He only spoke to me like it was just a matter of time.

Who were some of your earliest influences?

I was definitely influenced by Eddie [Murphy], but I was also influenced by Carlin and Pryor. I mean I was so green! Man, if you saw me, I was so green every week, I was influenced by somebody different. The night Eddie saw me, I was okay, in retrospect. At that time, I was like, "Oh my God." But again, every week I was influenced by some-body different. I'd be like, "Ooooh, look at that thing that Seinfeld's doing. I wanna be like that." And Kinison was a guy I'd watch either here or at Catch, and I'd be like, "What the fuck was that?" It was mind-blowing. It was kind of like being in school. I didn't realize I was at school, but I was. I was totally absorbing stuff, and it's weird 'cause I still know everybody's act.

Almost any guy I see or bump into, I can tell you a joke of his, and sometimes I'm hanging with [Adam] Sandler, or whomever, and we always start talking about old comedians, and we immediately go into somebody's act.

Who were some of the people you were coming up with? Do you remember any of them?

Sure. There was Jim Mendrinos. Jim was always here and was like the nicest guy. So especially late night it would be Jim Mendrinos, me, and Colin Quinn just hanging out. And that was the difference between me and a lot of other guys. They were here at the bar for free booze. I watched the shows and took it all in. I was really in the showroom most of the time.

Did Eddie tell you that night that he was gonna put you in a movie?

Naah, naah. He gave me his phone number, and said, "Hey, let's hang out." So then I think it was two nights later, we all went out together with his whole entourage, me and his mother, and whoever he was seeing at the time, we all went out to see this little movie by a new director named Spike Lee called *She's Gotta Have It.* It was that fucking long ago. Spike Lee was selling T-shirts in front of the theater.

Were you at all nervous to call him after he gave you his number?

I definitely was nervous to call him, and I wouldn't have ever called him if it wasn't for Louis Faranda, who was a bartender at Catch at the time. He told me to call. I told him about Eddie giving me his number, and he said, "So, are you gonna call?" I'm like, "Naaah, I'm not gonna call." And Louis said, "What, are you fuckin' crazy? Call him." I would have never called Eddie if Louis hadn't encouraged me.

What did your family think when you told them you were onstage, and Eddie Murphy liked you? Did they go crazy?

Not really. It was dismissed. It was like they were thinking, "He's probably lying or something." It wasn't their world. Brooklyn is maybe a forty-minute train ride, but it might as well be 3,000 miles away. You know, it's like, "What the fuck's a comedy club?" If you're not livin' in Manhattan, how are you gonna know what any of this stuff is? They were just so far removed.

And this whole thing happened really, really quick. I met Eddie on a Friday, went to the movies that Sunday, and my Dad, as I told you, drove a truck for *The Daily News*, so from Friday to Sunday it's all about the Sunday paper. We barely saw him. So maybe I told them about Eddie Murphy, but they had other things to think about.

So after the movie Eddie just says to me, "We're going to LA tomorrow, so if you wanna come, just come."

And did you go?

Hell yeah. I had never been on a plane before, certainly never went to LA before, and never stayed at a hotel before. They put us up at L'Hermitage, and every now and then I stay there.

Eddie was doing re-shoots for *Golden Child*, which he did in between *Cop 1* and *Cop 2*. He took me to the set with him and everything. In those days, I didn't even know what a "re-shoot" was.

And while I was out there, I actually auditioned for *The Tonight Show*. Eddie had Jim McCawley [the booker for the show], come down and see me, and I went up onstage at The Comedy Store, but I didn't get it. It was totally okay.

I remember Richie saying to me, "Hey kid, I got some bad news for you." He always called me "kid."

But to tell you the truth, it wasn't really bad news to me. *Please*, I had already won the lottery as far as I was concerned. Eddie Murphy took me out to LA and was putting me in his movie. How much more could I have wanted? If I had gotten *The Tonight Show* on top of that, it would have actually been too much!

But so far everything that's happened in my career, I've been like, "Okay, fine!" I might not have been here today with you guys if I had gotten *The Tonight Show* then. Who knows? My head might have fucking exploded! So, I wound up staying out there in LA for about two weeks.

So what's your life like when you come back from LA after shooting Beverly Hills Cop 2 *with Eddie Murphy?*

I came back to the clubs, and I immediately got good spots. I came back as a regular instead of a stand-by. I wasn't Joe Bolster, but I'd call up and put my availabilities in, and I had a spot almost every night, and I really got to develop onstage.

And the cool thing about this club was that it was packed every weekend. And maybe there were more people at Catch during the week, but this was the place to be on the weekend. Hands down, this place was the spot on the weekends.

What made this place so special?

There were just more blue-collar guys at The Strip. And I'm talking about both the audience and the performers. Everybody had a job. Catch was more Upper East Side. Here you got a lot of Queens and a lot of Bridge and Tunnel.[7] It was just a better mixture of people.

And during the week you had the freedom to actually work on shit. I mean, make sure you get offstage with a laugh, but you can't grow as a performer if you can't take a chance and bomb. That's how you grow. It wasn't like every set was an audition during the week. You had more freedom to try new things.

Any unusual Lucien stories, 'cause everybody seems to have at least one?

Lucien was just a very, very unique character. Felix Unger would be the closest thing if you were to try and think of a character from fiction. Try and imagine Felix Unger running a comedy club. And not just *any* comedy club. A club full of Oscar Madisons, 'cause that's basically what every comedian is.

---

[7] Queens and "Bridge and Tunnel" is a slang term referring to New Yorkers who don't live in Manhattan. They travel in by bridge and tunnel!

Richie and Lucien were great, 'cause in a weird way their dynamic influences people I myself hire to do shit today. Just think about it: Richie and Lucien, they had absolutely nothing in common. But they trusted each other. That was a revelation to me. And that is the most important thing at the end of the fucking day. Richie could literally be gone for months, but the club went on, and I'm sure the money was right and everything was cool. Trust and respect are the two most important things.

Who in a nightclub can you trust? How easy is it in a place like this to skim off the top? It's made for skimming. But Richie and Lucien trusted each other. One of the things I love about this business is the people it puts you in contact with that you would *never* have met in any other business. I just remember doing gigs like with me, Joy Behar, and Emo Phillips. What do these three people have in common? Nothing. Absolutely nothing. Less than nothing.

It's crazy. You just end up in cars taking rides with guys you just met to go someplace and tell jokes for fifty bucks. Where would I have ever met a guy like Lucien Hold? Maybe I would have cleaned up his house or something! How else would I ever have gotten to know him so well and be at his house and get to meet his family? Only in show business does that happen. To meet someone from such a different world and really get to know them well.

When did you meet Jerry Seinfeld and Paul Reiser and some of the original Comic Strip legends since they had already moved to LA by the time you got here?

Jerry would come back once in a while, whenever he could. So you'd see Jerry around town in between gigs. [Mario] Joyner was actually better friends with Jerry 'cause he actually opened for him at some gigs. And I remember being invited to come with them to The Green Kitchen.[8] It was like, "Hey, you can come too," that type of thing. "Oh, I can come

---

[8] The Green Kitchen is a twenty-four-hour diner on 77th and 1st where all the comics hung out.

to the diner with you?" And I'd just sit there and not say anything, just listening. And that was maybe '88 or '89.

I probably didn't have a real conversation with the guy till about '96. To this day, I always had a respect for people who were ahead of me. Success does not give you the right to treat people with less respect than they deserve.

So after you did Cop 2, *you had kind of a name in show business?*

Again, it's weird, when you finally get into show business. I guess it is a big credit to be in a movie like that if you're in The Comic Strip or Catch or some other club, but in the scheme of things, it's not that big a deal. My name also helped.

Yeah, Chris Rock is an unusual name.

Yeah, to me it was like Darryl Strawberry. It was the kind of name you don't forget. I lucked out with my name. But it was like the worst name growing up. Kids would throw rocks at me and call me Flintstones and Piece of the Rock. But for show business, it's the greatest name ever.

What were your first impressions of Richie Tienken?

It was kind of weird. First of all, he was kind of famous to me, 'cause "Hey, he was the guy from *Delirious,* who counts 'em down." So I had seen him in *Delirious* countless times. I saw it so many times, I know every beat.

And I think Richie was the only white guy in it, so he really stood out. Richie was always very "Colonel Tom Parker." They didn't look anything alike at all, but if Eddie was Elvis, which he was to a lot of people, then Richie was Colonel Tom. Absolutely! It was like, "The Colonel's here! Shape up!" Back then, Richie was managing literally the biggest star in the world. Not one of the biggest stars in the world, *the* biggest star.

Were people afraid of him?

Nah, it was weird. People were afraid of Wachs but not Richie. Nobody was afraid of Richie. Richie would actually talk to you. He'd be holding court with a bunch of the comics. He was like Big Paulie in *Goodfellows*. Everybody would come by Paulie's table and give respect. He was absolutely Paulie.

All Richie's dealings were with Lucien for the most part. Richie would come in, watch a couple of acts, and always have something good to say. Even if you bombed, he'd say something like, "Eh, next time kid." And he called everybody "kid," no matter how old you were. But it was never one of those things where anyone said, "Hey, the boss is here. Everybody's gotta behave." Lucien ran such a tight ship that Richie didn't have to bother with that. And Richie always had a new Cadillac.

Who was on SNL when you were on?

SNL was my big break. *Beverly Hills Cop 2* got me noticed in the clubs, but *SNL* was really my big break. Lorne [Michaels] was producing, and I was on with Adam Sandler, David Spade, Chris Farley, Rob Schneider, Phil Hartman, Kevin Nealon, Dennis Miller. We had a killer cast, and I was on there for three seasons, from like '91 to '93. But during that time, I'd still come into The Strip to work out stuff.

And then from *SNL* I went on to *In Living Color*, and I was out in LA for one season. I got there at the end. Literally, Jim Carrey had *Ace Ventura* come out that year, and once he was gone, they kind of pulled the plug on the show.

Any final thoughts about Richie?

All I know is hanging around Richie and hanging around the club, I got to see a lot of shit and saw a lot of shit to do and a lot of shit not to do. There'd be movie deals going on, and Richie would be screaming at Jerry Bruckheimer or something, or Katzenberg, or whatever, and I'd just be in the room like a fly on the wall.

And it was Richie who told me to pace the stage like a tiger when I perform, which is what I did in my HBO special *Bring the Pain*. Richie always said, "If you walk, people have to pay attention to you. If you stand in one place, they can talk to a friend, come back, and you're still where they left you. But if you keep moving, they have to pay attention to you." It's really very simple. It's a little thing, but you remember it, 'cause they have to pay fuckin' attention.

Any closing thoughts on The Comic Strip?

The Comic Strip is just a great room. There's something that happens here, especially Saturday night, first show in this room. And I'm sure I'm not the first guy to say that. Something about these ceilings . . . they're kinda low. The lights, the way they come up and back down again, the size of the room, it's nice and compact. I don't really know how to explain it, but all together it's something special.

And in this business that's so fuckin' cutthroat, people like to hang out here. It's nice that people always feel like they have a place like this to go. Look at D. F. [Sweedler] and J. J. [Ramirez]. They will always have a spot here, and that's pretty fantastic. That's why guys who have made it come back to visit. The Christmas party was always amazing. It was and is a very special place.

I've been very lucky. I'm in the middle of Bed-Stuy, in a very hostile environment, and I get these two great parents, Rose and Julius Rock. How the fuck did that happen? And then I'm in the middle of show business, and I get this lovely club that's nurturing in a business where *nothing* is nurturing!

Gilbert Gottfried[9]

Gilbert Gottfried is a comedian, actor, and voice-over specialist who is a regular on TV and in films such as *Beverly Hills Cop 2* and *The Aristocrats.* His performance as Iago, the wise-cracking parrot in Disney's *Aladdin*, made him one of the top voice over talents. He sells out venues across the country, and his new book, *Rubber Balls and Liquor*, is available now.

What are your earliest memories of The Comic Strip?

I never played The Comic Strip. I'm sorry. I just came for lunch. But I had heard it was in a building in Manhattan somewhere.

Thanks for the interview, that was wonderful.

It had a door and a window, and I think it had its name outside. And then men came there and said words, and people responded by moving their bodies up and down and making sounds.[10]

Seriously, Gilbert, tell me something about The Comic Strip and your comedy career.

I had been doing comedy for a number of years. The first major club was The Improv. I had started performing for the first time when I was about fifteen, and it was at The Bitter End. I would go anywhere where

---

[9] This interview was done at Pastis because Gilbert felt that it would be good to do an interview in one of the noisiest places in Manhattan during lunchtime, so that basically we had to scream to be heard.
We had to pick him up at his house to make sure he got there. In the car, we reminisced about the time we did a film together that I had written for The Playboy Channel called *Seeing is Believing*, in which he appeared with Camille Donatacci, who later went on to become Camille (Mrs. Kelsey) Grammar from the *Real Housewives of Beverly Hills*. In the movie, Gilbert played a guy trying to get contact lenses with X-ray vision so he could see through women's clothing, and she played the sexy nurse whose clothing he tried to see through!

[10] At this point Richie began to look nauseated as he realized he had just paid forty dollars to park and was paying for lunch, and Gilbert was insisting he was never there!

I was lucky enough not to get paid. I would basically work anywhere at all, as long as they promised not to pay me. "Hey there's no money here. I'll be right over."

So I'd been playing a bunch of clubs and then Catch A Rising Star opened, and I started playing there. There were millions of small clubs. Basically, anyone who had a bar was trying to have comedy there. Some of the places didn't even have mics; you had to yell out your jokes. And you'd stand up on some box or something.

By the time The Comic Strip opened, I was already known so I didn't have to audition for Lucien, who was an odd character.

What I liked best about The Strip was that it was about three blocks from Catch, so you didn't even have to pay for a bus. In those days, walking was still free, not like now where there's a tax on walking. So I'd walk back and forth.

When The Strip first started, they had three revolving hosts—and they actually did revolve. No one had ever seen anything like that before, and it got lots of customers to come in. They kept them in a glass case, like pies in a Greek diner, and people would come in and say, "I'd like to try that host please."

Two of the three revolving hosts went out of their minds, literally. They went crazy. There was Larry Cobb and Bob Getty. I had heard that both of them tried to commit suicide.

This was before they heard your act or afterwards?

During.

So what happened with The Comic Strip?

I got there a few years before it opened and stood out in the street waiting for it to be built. I kind of figured out where the stage was going to be put, and I stood in that part of the street until the club was planned, built, and finished. I had a slight idea in my head where they might put the bar, and then I'd go over there and get a soda.

So there were three hosts, two went nuts. Larry Cobb actually killed himself. He seemed a very straight-laced kind of guy, maybe a little high-strung, a little tight maybe, but my first thought on meeting him was not that someday he would probably kill himself.

He came over and asked me for career advice, and I told him to become homeless, live in the park, eat scraps out of the garbage, and eventually try and kill yourself. In retrospect, I probably should have suggested that he work on Wall Street or maybe in a store or something. I don't know. At the time it sounded right to me.

Now the other one I think tried to kill himself, but I don't think he was successful because he failed at everything.

Now what I remember most about The Comic Strip is more so than the other clubs, it seemed like Jerry Seinfeld was the star of The Comic Strip. And it seemed like 99 percent of the comedians who were Comic Strip regulars would talk exactly like him, male or female. They all started sounding just like Jerry Seinfeld. Even the girls.

Now in those days, before anyone really knew who he was, I would go onstage and do imitations of Jerry, and the comics would be cracking up, but the audience would be scratching their heads trying to figure out who I was doing.

I remember one time a club owner said to me, "Why are you doing Seinfeld? Do someone that people actually know." I had been doing impressions since the time I started, when I was around fifteen.

And sometimes, I used to paint onstage. I didn't do impressions like Jimmy Cagney or anything. I would do actual paintings in the Impressionistic style, and sometimes it would take about five days and the audience was very patient and they just sat and watched.

So other people who worked there were Paul Reiser, Larry Miller, George Wallace—the governor not the comedian. He used to stand outside the club and make sure no blacks could come in. Then there was Carol Leifer, who was easier to get into than any of the clubs, and who were some of the others?[11]

I'm interviewing you. You can't interview me.

No, it's okay. I'm gonna take a nap now. I wanna hear what you know about The Comic Strip.

What were your feelings about Lucien?

If I say someone's a little odd, you can only imagine. I'm still convinced he was gay, and I don't care what anyone says. And even if he never had any gay sex, he should have because I say he was gay. He would just kind of stare at you. He never seemed to smile or anything. He had one look on his face that he gave you, and it made you very uncomfortable.

Can you think of anything funny or unusual that happened to you as a result of working at The Comic Strip?

No.

Do you even know that you're here today?

No, but I had a nice lunch.

When did you get SNL?

I was on *SNL* I think between '80 and '81. I had been working the clubs, and after *SNL* I just went back to the clubs. I had gone to an audition at Catch, and I was doing Willy Loman in *Death of a Salesman,*

---

[11] It was important to Gilbert that readers know he was just kidding about Carol Leifer and that he has a lot of respect for her. It was just a funny joke.

and then eventually I went to doing the leads. Jean Doumanian was the producer.

They picked me for the show, and unfortunately I got it. I was on with Eddie Murphy and Joe Piscopo, and this was so long ago that Eddie was white. He hadn't developed that whole black character yet. It was very early in his career.

In The Comic Strip, they had a little table and chair and that was also very important for your readers to know.

Do you have any stories about Larry Miller?

He was there.

How about George Wallace?

He was tall.

How about Richie Tienken. What did people say about him in those days?

Also gay. I can actually say I was in a movie with Richie Tienken. I was in *Beverly Hills Cop 2,* and Richie pops up in the end. And I can't even say I got that part through Eddie. Surprisingly, Eddie told me that the first day I was on set, he was looking at the call sheet, and he was surprised to see my name there. So he didn't even know.

So how did you get the part?

I blew Judge Reinhold.

From what you said earlier about Bob Wachs's influence, I thought you were going to say it was thanks to Bob Wachs.

Well, actually Bob Wachs directed the film. He gave the credit to Tony Scott, but he was actually the one who directed it. Basically, everyone in Hollywood owes their careers to Bob Wachs. Even candles that are made out of "wachs" owe that to Bob Wachs. The movie *House of Wax* was thanks to Bob Wachs. Any time you "wax prolific," it's thanks to Bob Wachs. When you're lying in bed by yourself, and you give yourself a few whacks, it's actually a tribute to Bob Wachs, who invented jerking off. He's also responsible for the bikini wax.

Is there anything about Bob Wachs that we missed in this interview?

No.

Did you attend the memorial service for Lucien?

No, I was getting a free lunch that day.

How did you make the transition to film? What was the biggest thing that took you out of the clubs and got you to a movie set?

It was a car. They sent it for me, and it took me right there.

Please give me a statement of what The Comic Strip meant to you before Richie goes berserk.

I think they had popcorn, and I happen to like popcorn. So that was good. And sometimes I could walk behind the bar and use the soda hose. Not to drink soda out of it. I would have sex with it.

I remember that one of the bartenders used to do impressions, and one day he was doing something straight out of Rich Little's act. So I asked him, "Isn't that from Rich Little's act?" And he said, "Oh, Rich gave it to me. He said I could have it." And I said, "Oh, all right. So you mean if you like something from another comics' act, sometimes they just give it to you? Oh, you like it? Okay, you do it."

Did they serve dessert at The Comic Strip, because I think that was a highlight for a lot of the comedians?

Yes, definitely. After a long day, many of the comics looked forward to coming to The Comic Strip to have dessert. And Lucien would serve the dessert. They even had Christmas parties then, usually around Christmas time. Sometimes they had them in March because it was cheaper. [Right in the middle of talking, Gilbert suddenly yelled out to no one in particular, "Bring me a Peach Melba!" and then went right back to talking.] And I used to go because they served free food.

The Comic Strip parties were about the comedians, more than Catch, where the comics would kind of stand off to the side. Not that The Comic Strip was more friendly to the comics, but they had a table with two chairs, and the comics would take turns sitting down. Now that I think back about it, they might have had two benches, not two chairs, that each accommodated two people.[12]

Any last words about The Comic Strip?

In all seriousness, I have nothing to say about The Comic Strip! I would like to thank it for having a stage and for having electricity, because working without those two things can be very difficult, and I would have to say that The Comic Strip had the best electricity of any club I ever worked at.

Can you say one nice thing about the club?

It's a wonderful club, and if I had ever worked there, I'm sure I would have liked it immensely. But I do like Richie Tienken. In all the years I knew him he never hit me even once, and one time he even gave me a glass of water. Make sure you say that!

---

[12] At that point, Gilbert asked if he could take a quick pee. He explained that he was older than he was when he started at The Comic Strip and needed to pee more often. He explained that thinking about the years that went by made you have to pee really badly. When he came back from the restroom, we reminisced about the time Gilbert's appendix burst and he almost died. He explained that he was too cheap to go to a doctor and tried removing it himself, with the assistance of his mother, but it didn't go all that well.

Jackie Martling

Known best as Jackie "The Jokeman" Martling, he was Howard Stern's head writer for fifteen years, through four television series and three pay-per-view specials. He's also an actor, a producer, and a comedian who performs nationally as a headliner.

So when did you start performing, and what are your earliest memories of The Comic Strip?

I was a rock-and-roll musician in the '70s, and I was terrible. I graduated from Michigan State College in 1971 as a mechanical engineer, and I played rock and roll all through high school and college. I had a rock-and-roll band before The Beatles came. Then I came back from college and started playing on Long Island. It was me and another guy, and we told jokes, fooled around, played original songs, and we called ourselves Off Hour Rockers.

So there was a place in Oyster Bay called Rum Runner. It was a rock club, and we used to play there to 500 people, and they'd charge them a dollar a head to get in, and we would get the door. And I could still remember that was more than we had made anywhere else.

So the word got out that there were 500 people on Tuesday nights in Oyster Bay, and half of them were broads, so every horny bastard used to come out there, including Peter Bales, who lived in Locust Valley and who was a Comic Strip act. He was one of the guys that dated Carol Leifer and was one of the original Seinfeld, Larry Miller, Paul Reiser guys, that era of comics.

Anyway, he found out that we were doing the shows and there was a place called My Father's Place in Roslyn, Long Island, and everybody worked there, like Springsteen and The Rolling Stones, and it was really a big deal to get booked there. It was a show club.

And we got booked there. It was like two guys hittin' their heads with spoons, and I'm tellin' you the place would rock. And we were doing so good we couldn't believe it. We used to go into the liquor store and buy a bottle of each kind of booze, and we'd raffle them off from the stage, which was so illegal.

They had *The Gong Show* auditions at My Father's Place in those days, and one night I saw two guys perform, and one guy gets up and he's not really funny, and then another guy gets up and he's a little funnier, and it turns out it's Jim Myers and Richie Minervini.

And I grab Minervini and I said, "Why don't you stick around and watch us?" So he did, and he said, "You know what, you're funnier than I am. Why don't you be a comedian?"

Now, I had never thought of being a comedian. I thought you had to be anointed or something. I didn't know you could just choose to become one. I said to him, "How do you become a comedian?" He said, "Easy. I had cards printed up!" And I swear, he hands me a card that I still have to this day, and it said, "Come to Richard M. Dixon's White House Inn."

This was the place where Eddie Murphy started when he was fifteen years old.

I had a little XLR amplifier that you could plug a mic into, so from the first night I put up speakers and a recorder and I started recording my sets, and within six months, I put out my first album. I made them myself. Me and Minervini produced these shows, the audience was paying three bucks, and me and Minervini split the profits.

Then it was Peter Bales who insisted that I come down to The Comic Strip and audition for Lucien. So he literally dragged me in here, and

I auditioned for either Lucien or Richie, and they told me afterward it was a little too heavy on the fart stuff, but they kind of liked me. I came back again, and they told me I passed.

Then they called me and told me I was on the schedule and I told them, "I can't come into The Comic Strip." You wouldn't believe how many shows I was producing. I didn't have time.

So one day I got a call that someone got sick and they called me at the last minute, that they needed someone at The Comic Strip in Fort Lauderdale, and I thought to myself, "This is my chance." After one show, Joe Mullen [the manager] said to me, "Wow!" He loved me 'cause I was built for raucous audiences.

Joe used to come in and watch my show, and he'd go, "Jackie will not be denied," 'cause if they didn't laugh I'd go, "You mother fuckers!" And I'd intimidate them into laughing.

Now in those days when the comics would fly down to perform, Richie put them up in what was known as The Comedy Condo. Richie had either bought or rented a beautiful condo on Sunrise, thinking that the comics were young gentlemen who would respect it and take care of it. And after two weeks or a month, these comics were such drunken, disgusting slobs that they got thrown out and they got moved to a duplex somewhere else, which they continued to call The Comedy Condo.

Around Easter of 1980, I hadn't worked The Comic Strip yet, but I had gotten friendly with Rodney Dangerfield. I had been badgering him for a while, ever since I got him the "two-bagger" joke.

You wrote the "two-bagger" joke?[13]

I didn't write it, I got it to him. That's what's known as comedy writing. I found half of Rodney's act in Gershon Legman's book, like, "My wife cut

---

[13] The joke, as I recall, was, "I was with this girl who was so ugly, I call her a two bagger. That's where you put a bag on your head, in case the bag on her head breaks."

me down to twice a week. That's not bad. I know a couple of guys she cut out all together." That was a joke about two black guys talking to each other from 1863. Rodney adapted it to his act.

So I was begging Rodney to take me away with him, so one day he calls me up and says, "Hey, you wanna go to Vegas? I'm headlining The Aladdin." Then he adds, "You like Lauderdale? I'm stopping off there too, taking my daughter on vacation. You come there too, okay?" So I flew down with Rodney's daughter Melanie and her girlfriend Debbie, who were about sixteen in those days, rented a car, got them situated at the Bahia Mar hotel, and then went back to get Rodney.

Rodney and I go out to see Louie Nye, with Rodney's daughter and son, and Louie comes over after the show, and I convince them all to go to The Comic Strip. I hadn't been to Lauderdale since I was in college, but I got them in my car, and I'm trying to find the place.

Finally, we found the place. I pull up, and I'll never forget this. Even though I hadn't played The Comic Strip yet, I knew all these guys from booking them: Dennis Wolfberg, Larry Miller, Bob Nelson, Peter Bales, Glenn Hirsch, Paul Reiser, and it was between shows, so everyone was hanging out, and I walk in with Louie Nye and Rodney, and Richie was shocked, and he says to Rodney, "Hey, remember when we met in Las Vegas and you called me The Silver Fox?" Richie always had a warm spot for me for being the guy who brought Rodney to the club. And Rodney said, "Hey, they comped the whole thing. That was really nice."

Go back to how you made the transition from music to comedy.

In 1979, I was in a three-piece band, and after one of our shows two of the guys come up to me and go, "You know, Jackie, we're gonna leave the band and start our own band." And I said to myself, "I'm not a rocket scientist, but if there's three guys in the band, and two of them leave to start their own band, that's kicking me out of the fucking band!"

But the truth of it was, they didn't really kick me out, 'cause it was my songs, my stories, so that's when I started playing by myself, and that's when I met Minervini and those guys. I had nothing else to do. My songs weren't any good, I wasn't any good at music, and I had no band. The only thing I had left was to tell my stupid jokes onstage.

When I first showed up at Catch in 1978, I tried putting together a monologue, but it was so horrible. Even after I passed at The Comic Strip on my second audition, I didn't come back for a long time. I didn't do the clubs to try and get my seven minutes for TV, because my act was not made for TV. I just tell dirty jokes. I was mostly a producer, and I was also working as a studio manager in a recording studio.

So I worked all over and made money. In August of 1980, I worked every single night, seven days a week.

So one night in the early '70s, I went into Catch A Rising Star. I had read in the paper how on Monday nights, people went in and waited on line to perform, and I thought to myself, "That oughta be interesting."

So me and my sister's boyfriend, Archie, went and sat right in front of the stage, and people are doing their five minutes and someone got up and did two minutes, panicked, and ran off the stage. The MC was gone and some drunken broad jumped up onstage and told some horrible joke but brought the house down, because the previous three or four acts had been so bad.

The MC comes back and, I think it was Kelly Rogers, and then David Sayh took over and the same thing happened. The comic left the stage in about fifteen seconds, and nobody's onstage, so my pal Archie encourages me to get up onstage. So I was drunk and I got up and told the oldest, dirtiest joke I knew and really brought the house down.

Better than that, as I was walking out, David Sayh stopped me and said, "That was a really funny joke, man. Did you ever think about doin' this?"

Now I grew up on Long Island, so I just figured that everyone knows all the jokes that I know, 'cause we're all from the same area, but if I told that joke in Manhattan and it brought the house down, and the MC from Catch didn't know that joke, maybe there are other people who haven't heard that joke, so the light bulb went off, and I just started telling my dirty jokes. Nobody else was doin' it, and I love doin' it.

What did you think of Richie when you first met him?

I thought we had an immediate zap. I think we liked each other right away. I knew right away that I didn't like Lucien, but I knew right away that I liked Richie 'cause we're the same guy. I think he realized I wasn't the hippest act in the world, but I was the nicest guy in the room. Like, "I don't know if I want this guy in my club, but I could certainly have some fun with him." That type of thing!

Susie Essman

Susie Essman is a comic, actress, and author, and is probably best known these days for playing the character of Susie Greene in HBO's hit series *Curb Your Enthusiasm*. Her book, *What Would Susie Say–Bullshit Wisdom About Love, Life and Comedy*, is a best seller.

When did you start performing, and what are your earliest memories of The Comic Strip?

I started performing at the very end of 1983, and I passed at The Comic Strip in 1984. The Comic Strip was actually pivotal in my stand-up career.

When I first started, I started working at a club downtown that opened in 1983 called Comedy U. It was on University and 13th Street. My first performance ever was in July of 1983, I got up at an open mic night at a place called Mostly Magic on Carmine Street. There that night were Bert Levitt and Paul Herzich, and they came up to me, and it never even occurred to me to be a comic . . . I thought I was going to be a comedic actress like a Carol Burnett or a Lily Tomlin, just doing characters. So these guys came up to me after my very first performance, and they said, "We're opening a club in a couple of months, we loved you, and we want you to work at our club."

I gave them my number and never thought I would hear from them, but a few months later I get a call: "We opened a club. Can you come to the club and do ten minutes?" I didn't have ten minutes. Ten minutes to me back then might as well have been six hours.

But of course I didn't tell them that. And I hadn't been onstage since that one night. You know it's funny, but now that I think about it, if it wasn't for those guys, I don't know that I would have become a comic. Anyway, I said, "Okay, I'll come in," and I quickly wrote ten minutes of material.

Now in those days, all I did was characters. It took me a long time until I spoke in my own voice. I used to do my grandmother, my mother, anybody but myself, especially if they had a Jewish accent. I didn't do impressions; I did real people. I still do that today. But in those days, I was so afraid to speak that's all I did. I had material in the characters, but it was always done in the character's voice.

So I wrote ten minutes, went down there on a Sunday night, and they invited me to come back on a Thursday night, which was their all-female comedy night. As a matter of fact, that's where I met Joy Behar, who's still my best friend today. Comedy U on a Thursday night. It was Rita Rudner, Carol Leifer, Marion Allen, who I don't know if you knew. She was a great comedian . . . a very, very funny comedian who left the business because, as you know, this business is not for everyone.

So Marion Allen and Scott Blakeman used to work at The Comic Strip, and they were the ones that kind of talked me into coming up here. And when I came uptown a couple of times with Marion it made me realize I had to start developing more of an act, and I can't just do these characters.

So I came uptown one night and auditioned for Lucien. Marion and Scott had both told him about me, and a couple of other people from Comedy U had mentioned me. He passed me on my first time.

Now I had heard from other people, like Patty Rosborough, that Lucien was the scariest person in the whole world, but for some reason he took to me. Lucien was definitely not scary to me. We immediately had a rapport.

When I first started working here, Colin Quinn was a bartender. He was not a comedian yet, and I always remember telling him, "You know, you really are so funny. You really have to do this." So anyway, Lucien passed me and very quickly started giving me what you might call very "protected" kind of spots. Like he might put me on first on a Saturday night. He'd never put me on at three o'clock in the morning when there were animals loose in the club.

He watched over me. And even though some people might think that being first to go up is also a hard spot, let me say that if you have a good MC, it's not that hard. They already warm up the audience and get them in a good mood.

So, a great MC really helps the show. And Lucien . . . there were so many Lucien stories because he was such an eccentric, idiosyncratic kind of guy. But the thing about Lucien that I always had tremendous admiration for was that he was the most honest person I have ever met. If you auditioned for Lucien, he might very well say to you, in that unique voice of his, "Well, you're not funny, and I have no use for you at this club." And people left here in tears, but the truth is, he was almost always right.

He was not funny himself, but he knew funny when he saw it.

And he was extremely loyal. If he liked you, and he thought you were funny, that was it. You were in. Forever. So then I started working at The Strip a lot, and that's when I really started to develop as a comic. And he was so good to me, and I never slept with him!

He was married to Michelle at the time. And Richie and Bob were not around much since Eddie Murphy was already on *SNL*, but Richie was like a rock star. He was like a god. People were in awe of him. He would just like saunter in, and people would be like, "Who's this man with the big mane of white hair?" And honestly, I was a little scared of Richie, just 'cause there was like this aura about him, and I was kinda new and nervous . . . like a little virgin.

I remember actually my first weekend spot here. 'Cause getting a weekend spot was a big deal, 'cause that's where you made fifty bucks. That was a lot of money, and in those days I used to just run around to all the clubs, seven or eight shows a night, and that was my rent by the end of the weekend. All the clubs paid about the same. Some clubs may have paid sixty dollars per set, but MCs got even more.

I remember that Catch paid one hundred dollars, so they probably paid the same thing at The Strip, and my rent was 300 bucks a month, so I might have even had a little left over for food.

But wherever I went, I tried to arrange it geographically. Like I'd do a Comic Strip set, then I'd do a Catch set. Then I'd go downtown and do The Duplex, The Comedy Cellar, and Greene Street. Then I'd go to the West Side and try to get company, 'cause you didn't want to spend the extra cab fare.

So you'd be like, "Who's going where I'm going?" so you could share a cab. Unless you were Gilbert [Gottfried], then you take the bus!

But I used to try and plan my sets so that my last set would be at The Strip, 'cause then we'd all go to the diner. We'd either go to Gracie Mews, which was kind of The Comic Strip hangout, or else we'd meet up with the people from Catch and go to The Green Kitchen.

Then we'd stay at the diner till like five or six in the morning. We weren't big drinkers, really. The Catch crowd was more of the "druggy" crowd. The Comic Strip was more of the jocks. The Improv was more of those dark, cerebral kind of guys like Robert Klein and Larry David.

Larry was definitely an Improv act. I didn't actually meet Larry till a little later on, maybe 1987. But The Comic Strip crowd was the jocks because Lucien was a sports lover. He was a dancer, but he loved baseball. He was such a strange juxtaposition of things. But this was home. It was *haimishe* [Yiddish for comfortable].

You knew all the waitresses, you knew all the bartenders, and you knew all the comics. There weren't that many of us. It was like coming home to your family.

And then we formed an improv group here, The Comic Strip Improv Group, and we used to perform one night a week. I forgot what night it was; it could have been Monday. But it was me and Scott Carter, who's now the executive producer of the *Bill Maher* show, and Steve Heitner, and a whole bunch of us, and Lucien was very supportive of us. We would come here during the day to rehearse. We did an hour show and drew great audiences, and that was Lucien's baby, the Improv group.

And I really think that I learned my improvisational skills there, which I now use onstage and in *Curb* [*Curb Your Enthusiasm*]. I don't wanna sound goofy, but we were young and having a blast, and it was just like, "Hey kids, I got a barn! Let's put on a show!"

There was so much going on in the industry, like Robert Morton would come in to see people for the *Letterman* show, or Jim McCawley would come in for *Johnny Carson*. You never knew when some important industry people would be there, so you needed to be on the lineup all the time. And that was up to the creative director, which in the case of The Strip was Lucien.

For the first couple of years, I only worked The Comic Strip. It became clear to me that Catch would be a good place for me to get into career-wise, but The Strip was more of my safety club and my home. Catch was completely intimidating to me, and nobody would pass me there. Finally Cynthia Coe, whose title was director of artists management, came in to run Catch.

She liked me a lot. I think she saw me at Carolines, opening for Jerry Seinfeld. So I said to Joy Behar, "You know what? I'm just gonna act as if I passed. I'm gonna put in my availability," 'cause I was working a lot of clubs at the time, and they just started putting me up. It was the most amazing thing. No one ever asked if I had been formally passed.

Did you ever get anything particularly special as a result of working The Strip?

Absolutely! One Saturday night in 1986, I was onstage at The Strip MCing, and David Seltzer, who directed *Punchline*—the movie about stand-up comics—was in the audience with Sally Field. They were looking for comics for the movie, and they saw me and he called me the next day and offered me the job of Sally's coach, 'cause she was playing the part of a stand-up comic. Not her coach in the movie. Her coach to get her ready for the movie!

Next thing I knew, I was in Los Angeles on the Columbia Pictures lot working with Sally Field and Tom Hanks every day. And that was a direct result of me working The Comic Strip.

Tom Hanks was not as big a star at the time as he is now. He had done a couple of movies, like *Splash*, but he was an up-and-coming star. He would come with me to make the rounds of the clubs, and Tom would actually get up and do the material.

Any funny Lucien stories?

You know there used to be a thing; we all used to hang out here like Joe Bolster, Colin, and me, and a whole bunch of us, and the last thing you wanted to do was get stuck in a conversation with Lucien. 'Cause he would do what I would call "eyeball" you. He would lock eyes with you and monologue for months, and you couldn't get away. So we would have like a whole thing that if you saw Lucien in conversation with one of your friends, somebody would yell out, "Susie, you got a phone call," or something to let the person get away, and that's how we would save each other. But then the other person who saved you might get stuck, locked in conversation with Lucien. We would basically sacrifice ourselves for our friends, and we took turns doing that.

Lucien was proud of my success, but I think almost a little resentful that I didn't come around as much. I think he felt a little hurt that I was no longer hanging out at the club as much as I did before my career started taking off.

I never had any bad incidents with Lucien, but you can ask other comics about things he said to them that were absolutely brutal. Luckily, I never had any kind of experience like that. I was always extremely close with him.

I had two major things that happened to make my career. One, if Paul Herzich hadn't seen me that one night I performed at Mostly Magic and invited me to perform at Comedy U, I might never have had a comedy career. And the second thing was, if not for The Comic Strip I don't know where my career would have been. Comedy U was where I took my very first baby steps as a comedian, but The Comic Strip was the place where I learned my craft and found my comedic voice.

I would say that I have had some of the best sets in my life on this stage right here. Before I was some kind of esoteric downtown character, doing all character work as my act. I came to The Comic Strip, and I became a comic. I learned how to speak onstage here in my own voice.

We used tape recorders in those days too. It's funny 'cause I was great about taping. I just wasn't good about listening to them afterward.

But Lucien also had a videotape machine going, so you could also videotape your act to review it.

When did you first meet Larry David, a guy who has had such a big impact on your career?

I met Larry at Catch in the late '80s, 'cause that's where he worked. He was definitely a Catch act. We were kind of friendly in those days. He liked my act and would give me a compliment now and then, and we were friendly at the bar.

But in later years, he happened to see me perform at The Friars Roast of Jerry Stiller on Comedy Central, and that's when he got the idea to use me on *Curb*. He called me up and offered me the job of Susie Greene. All as a result of a Friars Roast.

Jeff Garlin I knew from The Strip. We used to work here together and hang out. We were always buddies. I had kind of lost touch with him too for a while, 'cause you know a lot of people move out to LA, and it makes it harder to stay in touch. But we were always close.

Any great stories you can think of before we finish?

I remember my first Saturday night spot. Jerry was here that night. He already lived in LA, but he had a place over on West 81st that he shared with George Wallace. I remember I was standing at the side bar telling Jerry it was my first weekend spot, and Jerry said to me, "Wow, you're really nervous." And I'm like, "Yeah, I'm *really* nervous." And Jerry said, "What are you so nervous about? You're so funny." And in my head I'm going, "Oh my God, Jerry Seinfeld told me that I was funny." Just thinking back about that now is so crazy. I was so impressed that Jerry Seinfeld complimented me.

If I could wrap it up, the thing about The Comic Strip is that I was "allowed," so to speak, to become a comic here, because I was made to feel safe enough that I could take chances and develop. I knew that even if I had a bad set, I could still always get a spot. That kind of safety net is invaluable to a comic, and it's what helped me become who I am.

Tony D'Andrea[14]

Tony D'Andrea is a former bartender currently working as an impressionist in Las Vegas. He was responsible for The Comic Strip being born.

What does The Comic Strip mean to you?

It's amazing that I was the inspiration for this club, but it's absolutely true. I wasn't even looking for a comedy club. This was around 1975, and I had been working for Richie for a couple of years already. I was his bartender, but I was also doing impressions. When Richie bought the Bull and Bush, I stayed with him 'cause I liked the guy. He was always a lot of fun. We packed 'em in. Not "packed in," where you can make tons of money. It was just plain packed, and Richie was satisfied with that.

One night I go downtown, and I get in line to perform at Catch A Rising Star.

After a couple of weeks I told Richie, "You gotta come down and see me." On a Monday night he walks in the joint, and you can't get in.

---

[14] Most readers may not be familiar with the name Tony D'Andrea, but if it wasn't for Tony, The Comic Strip might never have existed. Tony D'Andrea is a real Damon Runyan character, and I mean that in the best sense of the word. Now he's a successful Vegas impressionist, but back in the day, he was a bartender working for Richie Tienken in Tienken's Bronx bar, The Bull and Bush.

From the front door to the showroom, it's completely jammed. Wall to wall people.

So Richie, bein' a businessman says, "You mean to tell me that none of these comics get paid?" I said, "That's correct." He said, "I wonder how long it'll take us to open a joint." That was it, word for word. The Gospel truth. And then it happened. We opened this place here, and I was the bartender/comic, and I caught my break about two or three years after that.

Tell me more about how The Strip influenced you.

I worked here three to four nights a week as a bartender, and every one of those nights I got up and performed. I would tend bar, do the show, and come back behind the bar. Lucien was here at the time, and he knew Richie was my best friend, and he still gave me a hard time most of the time. Like I just finished my set, and if you do twenty minutes here, it takes a comic a good fifteen, twenty minutes to come down.

So one night I had an agent here from the Raleigh Hotel up in the Catskills who wanted to talk to me. So the guy's talkin' to me and Lucien comes over yelling, "Hey, I told you to get back behind the bar," and I came that close to knockin' him into next week. It was kind of rude of him, but I went back behind the bar. But if anyone ever came close to death . . . look at me [and at that he grabbed my face and pointed it towards him to make a point], if anyone ever came close to death, it was him. In general he was a nice guy, but I didn't care for the guy too much.

Richie is my lifelong friend. I'm godfather to his two kids, been with him forty years, and I never left him. I didn't wanna go with those other guys. He didn't know I was gonna be a comic, and I didn't know he was gonna buy the bar. He just had a likeable quality and something just told me, "Stay with this guy." And I've been with him like forty years . . . and he never even bought me dinner!

Eddie Brill

Eddie Brill is an internationally known stand-up comic who has taped more than a hundred TV shows in six countries. He was the talent coordinator for *The Late Show with David Letterman* for fourteen years and is currently the audience warm-up comedian.

What year did you start performing, and what were some of your earliest memories of The Comic Strip?

Well, I started in the '70s in Boston while I was in at Emerson College. My first ever New York experience was auditioning at The Comic Strip. And there were more comics than there were audience members.

I brought a friend with me, which really doubled the audience, and Eddie Murphy, who was also kind of starting out, was onstage that night. This must have been around 1979 or 1980. I was very nervous because I made a big deal that it was New York instead of just going and acting like it was a regular comedy club. Needless to say, because I was very scared, I didn't do very well.

I don't even remember who auditioned me. It was probably Richie, but I'm sure Lucien was there too. I didn't really get to even meet the person, because I did so bad that I just left as soon as I was done.

So I went back to Boston where I was comfortable. Then, I moved to New York where I quit doing stand-up comedy until 1984. In that year, I had the opportunity to manage a comedy club of my own, called The Paper Moon, in the West Village.

A friend of mine I went to college with was working as a waiter upstairs in the cabaret, and he told me they wanted to put in a comedy club downstairs. At the time, The Strip, The Improv, and Catch were the three big clubs in New York, but all the guys I knew from Boston and LA, San Francisco, and Chicago were not really getting stage time. So I wound up turning The Paper Moon into a headliner club with friends like Steven Wright, Bobcat Goldthwaite, and Jake Johannsen.

But I wanted to work the big clubs too, and they weren't really answering my phone calls, mostly because I had my own club. Then, around 1986, I got an audition for *Star Search*, a big TV show at that time. Claudia McMahon, Ed's daughter, was scouting for the show and saw me performing and asked if I'd like to audition for the show.

So she asked me where I wanted to audition, and because The Comic Strip was one of the most incredible clubs in the world, I wanted to go there . . . also to try and erase the bad memory they had of me.

Believe it or not, they still remembered my horrible audition from years before when I was so nervous and just starting out, and because of that I still wasn't able to perform there. So anyway, I requested that spot for my audition, thinking that now they could see how I improved.

Well, she said okay, and I auditioned for her at The Strip and had one of the best sets of my life. It was magical. Everything worked. Not only did I get *Star Search,* but I got booked forever and ever and ever from that day on at The Comic Strip. It turned out to be one of the greatest days of my life, and I'll never forget it.

One of the greatest stories of my life, and there are a million of them, is that the rule at The Comic Strip was that you'd go onstage if there's people in the audience. Even if there was one person, you go out there and do your act like it's a full room.

And I learned that from David Brenner earlier . . . one night I was at Carolines, and there were only like fourteen people in the audience at the headliner show, at twelve-thirty a.m., and I didn't really want to perform for so few people, and he said to me, "What kind of attitude is this? This is where I get my best sets. You work the crowd. They came to see *you*. Don't be mad at them, they're here." And I never forgot that lesson, and it was Brenner who taught me that.

Anyway, when I moved to Los Angeles, I gave Paper Moon to Rick Messina [who became Drew Carey's manager]. And after only one week of doing it, he said to me, "Eddie, I think I'm gonna try this business. I think I'm gonna move to LA like you." Now Barry Katz [a manager] had previously said to me, "Why'd you give the club to Rick Messina?" I said, "Because you live in Boston, and he lives in New York, and this is a New York comedy club." So when Rick gave it up, I said, "Barry, you run the club," and he called it the Boston Comedy Club.[15]

When did you leave Boston and start performing at the New York clubs on a regular basis?

While I was still at Emerson, I wound up working with Norman Lear to start the first comedy writing department in America at Emerson. So after college was over in 1980, I stayed on to teach. Denis Leary, who was my roommate, and I were both teachers at the school. There were a million Emerson comics over the years, like Mario Cantone, Bill Burr, and Bill Dana, the legendary Jose Jimenes, who is actually working on the comedy archives for Emerson.

I was sitting in Boston and I thought, "You know, I'm a big fish in a very small pond, and I've gotta go to New York."

So I had an audition at The Improv, and I was treated so poorly by Silver Friedman that I actually quit comedy for three years until the scenario came up where a friend of mine from college said, "I know you

---

[15] Barry Katz went on to create the hit TV show *Last Comic Standing*.

ran the comedy group up in Boston, and we're considering doing a comedy night here at The Paper Moon. Would you be interested in running it?"

What happened with Silver was, truth be told, I wasn't a great comic, but I happened to have had a good set at The Improv that night, and when I came off she didn't say a word to me. I was dying to know what she thought. So, finally I approached her, and she said, "I have nothing to say to you." And that was it.

I was shocked. And I had to actually go up to her and ask her for that. She didn't volunteer it on her own. But the interesting thing was that many, many years later, I was performing at Carolines at The Seaport, and I hear someone in the audience laughing and who does it turn out to be but Silver. So at the end of the show, she comes up to me and says, "Eddie, that's one of the funniest shows I've ever seen," and I looked her right in the eye and said, "I have nothing to say to you!" And I turned around and walked away.

In those early days who were some of your peers at The Strip?

Because I was from Boston, I really only knew Susie Essman and Colin Quinn, and especially since at my club I was using all the comics from Boston, LA, San Francisco, and Chicago, comics I knew from working on the road, I didn't hang with many New York comics. But there were so many people there at The Strip that I admired. They used to use the term "technicians," and there were so many of them at The Strip. There was Seinfeld and Reiser—guys I just loved.

Another thing that Lucien was famous for was putting the best show together. He had the best comic following the best comic, with a purpose, not just throwing someone on there for no reason. If you said you couldn't do the nine-fifteen, Lucien would say, "Well I'm sorry, you're the comic who needs to go on next. This is where I need you on the show." His shows would run impeccably.

Tell me about Richie Tienken.

The funny thing is that in the early days, I didn't get to know Richie Tienken that well. I watched him from afar. He always had all these talented, incredible guys around him.

We always said "hi," but I didn't really get the chance to know him well until later on. I don't know why I was that guy, but I was scared shitless of Richie Tienken!

Years later, I just happened to be sitting at the bar, and Richie was over there, and he turns around and we start talking, and I went home and thought to myself, "Gee, he's really a regular guy. What an asshole I've been."

Rick Overton

Rick is an actor/comedian and writer who believes that "one cannot attain true happiness without serotonin." An Emmy-award-winning writer for his work on *Dennis Miller Live*, his face has appeared in countless TV shows and movies, including *Groundhog Day. Willow*, and *Dinner for Schmucks*.

So when did you first start performing comedy, and what are your earliest memories of The Comic Strip?

I started performing in 1971, with a comedy team called Overton and Pastore. I was sixteen, in high school, and we were just playing coffee houses and dreaming of getting into New York and doing a team there. My partner was Tonn Pastore, who now lives in Florida.

After we broke up, I was still too insecure to perform alone, so this guy Bill Spitz, who I knew from a church organization I was in as a kid, introduced me to a guy named Rog Sullivan, who was this Marty Feldman kind of guy—mad, frizzy-haired cartoon of a guy and a genius . . . a Ferrari. I was more of an old Chevy.

But having a team just got impossible. It's the same amount of time for every act, but there's only one check that you gotta saw in half. Then there's that long drive where you gotta hear, "Well, my premise had more to do with it"; "No, my punchline was the reason we're onstage." It's hard splittin' money up. We did great when it was for free. Money causes too much pressure.

So we broke up in 1978, and I was scared. It was a long time for me saying a joke and twisting my head to the right. "No Rog. Hey, where did Rog go?" And I was the straight man!

So anyway, about The Comic Strip, Rog and I got spots every now and then at Catch and at The Improv, but The Comic Strip was really generous to us. We cut our teeth on The Strip, and I think we grew the fastest here. I started out there with Rog, but then, through my great fortune and happiness, they welcomed me back on my own too.

I was really scared I was done after Rog. I was wondering, "Does someone want half of a team?" But because of the generosity of Richie and Lucien, they all let me play and stretch on my own to find my own style and my voice. A lot of times, you get good because someone believed in you. It's like sunlight to a plant.

Comedians are "noticers," and noticers are sensitive. That's the little antenna on your little bug head that notices what's going on. If people beat the shit out of those antennae, it's like your TV—you can't get a good picture anymore. So, it was a terrifying journey from a two-man act to a one-man act, and thank God for improv, trying to remember like the way Jonathan Winters worked or how the new guy I just heard of, Robin Williams, was doing it. So at first I was able to do one or two bits I felt I had predominantly written myself in my solo act, but that soon fell away. Improv was writing a new act, and I had to trust it.

So when I came in to audition, Lucien was here and a guy named Ellis Levinson was MCing. I was out of the era of Elayne [Boosler] and Andy [Kaufman]—more at Catch too—but they also hung out here as well.

Who were so me of your contemporaries in those days?

John DiBellis would come in, and Seinfeld and Larry Miller and these were all guys I would hang out with a lot. A lot of people don't know that Larry Miller is also one of the greatest improvisers of all time. 'Cause what is your act? At any given point or moment of your life, you're doing either one of two things: You're either improvising or plagiarizing. There's no third option.

Tell me about Richie Tienken.

He fed us and we loved him. I had never seen such a loose, hip, crazy boss before. When I was just a plain working stiff, no bosses ever acted like that. I can promise you that. Richie just had a looseness about him that I thought was pretty cool. And we had a lot of fun when we hung out in Florida.

That was one of the great breaks they gave me to find my own speed and pace by sending me down to work the Fort Lauderdale club. That was the most amount of sex in one week with different people that I ever experienced. That was in the early '80s when we were doing Florida blow, and we still believed our tickers could take it. When Belushi died, I quit. But those were some crazy days.

The comedy condo. Holy shit. If there were hidden cameras in that place, it would have been like a 3,000-hour porn video. Sometimes strippers would come by and flash you during your show, and that was sort of a signal that you could have fun at the condo.

And the first few shows you do on cocaine are remarkable. That's not the point on the long run. It cooks out the remarkable device in you and you become pedestrian, and then you crash, and then you're stuck. But in the beginning it seems amazing, and your balls are fucking luminous, and they're made of stainless steel and bullet-proof and crowds respond to that, and you confuse that with good material.

Any stories about Lucien?

I'm so sad that he's gone. But he hung on and fought like a tiger too. They say he broke records for the illness in terms of endurance with scleroderma. This was his place. I was always proud that I could imitate his laugh. I try to do different comedians' laughs! [After which he broke into a loud, long-gapped-pause laugh with his head back like Lucien was prone to do.]

Wayne Federman

Wayne Federman is a comedian, actor, author, and comedy writer. He tours the country, often with Jimmy Fallon. He's been seen on *The X-Files*, *The Larry Sanders Show*, *Curb Your Enthusiasm*, *Legally Blonde*, *50 First Dates*, *The 40-Year-Old Virgin*, and *Step Brothers*.

When did you first come to perform at The Comic Strip?

I came to the club at a way different time than these other guys. My original goal was to be a stand-up comedian who could act. I came around in maybe '81 trying to get on, and at that time, Richie and Bob were already in LA with Eddie Murphy, so they were crazy, Hollywood, bright-light, movies-are-happening guys, and there was a lot going on, and it was very hard to pass at the club at the time.

I had originally come from Florida and went to NYU Drama School, and so I had never really heard of The Strip when I first got here. And I had read this book by a guy named Phil Berger called *The Last Laugh*, which was mainly about The Improv and comics like Jimmy [J. J.] Walker and Freddie Prinze, who hung out there, and so I wanted to see what The Improv was like. It seemed to be the gold standard of clubs at the time.

Then I heard about Catch and then The Strip, and apparently I was the first class that Lucien had passed, but I didn't actually pass until the end of '82. I had been working at places like The Tripple Inn and Who's On First that had opened up in Manhattan.

I had also been trying to curry favor with Bob and Richie, who didn't really have time for any of us. Richie would come in once a week, which I think was on a Monday night. He would be at the end of the bar doing the schedule, and when he was done, all the comedians would be standing around waiting and he'd throw the schedule down on the bar and go, "Read it and weep."

By the time I came, Seinfeld had already gone to California, but he would send postcards to the club with notes like, "Hey, I'm opening for Ann Murray in Vegas, these are the kind of crowds I've always dreamed of playing in front of, packed houses, and I really feel like I'm in show business." It was stuff like that to keep us informed of what he was doing, and we'd all gather around and read them around the podium. It was very interesting.

Reiser had just done *Diner* as a result of going with Michael Hampton Cain for an audition and Cain didn't get the role, but Reiser did. And Reiser said he was just expecting to go shopping for socks.

And unlike D. F. Sweedler, I was not invited to Lucien's parties right away. However Eddie Murphy's twenty-first birthday party was at Studio 54, and luckily I was on that list.

When I got here, MCs could no longer pass you to perform, and Peter Bales was one of the MCs who was here when I started out. If you weren't passed, he allowed you to come back in about three months to try again. And if he liked you, he'd recommend you to Lucien. It took me well over a year to get passed.

I was performing with Joe Bolster, D. F. Sweedler, Hiram Kasten, and Dennis Wolfberg, who actually had his own cup at the bar, which he drank out of. Dennis started out as a straight singer at first and used to sing "American Pie," but Larry Cobb accused him of doing that so that he could get better spots.

Then there was Steve Hytner, Barry Weintraub, and Colin Quinn was the bartender, and Lucien had a rule that if you worked in the club, you couldn't perform. So we encouraged Colin to quit the job so he could perform here.

As far as my fondest memories, I'd have to say the Christmas parties were very special because it wasn't just a party. People actually prepared special material for the party.

I went out to LA at the end of 1986, after having worked here for around five years, and this was my number-one club. And it was a very big deal for me to get booked into the Fort Lauderdale club.

Aside from getting invited to Lucien's party, getting a spot on New Year's Eve was also considered a feather in the cap of any comic who could get that. And as long as you were on the schedule here you were allowed to get a free cheeseburger, which was a big thing to us in those days.

D. F. Sweedler

D. F. Sweedler is a stand-up comic who has been performing at The Comic Strip since it opened in 1976. He also hosts shows there and teaches the comedy writing and performance classes.

As one of the originals here, what do you remember most about the early days?

My most indelible memory is that Richie used to beat me! Seriously, I performed on the second day the club opened, June 2, 1976.

I had been performing at Catch but very little, 'cause you could barely get on. There were a million comics, so maybe you'd get on and maybe you wouldn't. So one day I'm walking up 2nd Avenue, and I see a sign that there's another club opening, and I was like, "Wow, this is unbelievable." I was waiting outside the door before the club even opened.

So they had auditions for Bob and some woman who I don't remember. I came in in the afternoon, no audience, which is always the best way to audition for comedy, and Bob says to me, "Before you do this, I wanna show you how the shows are gonna start every night." So he turns on the fat lady. Did anyone mention the fat lady yet?

The fat lady was a wooden statue of a fat lady who rocked back and forth emitting loud laughter, and it was Bob's idea to start the show with that every single night. And I'm thinking to myself, "Holy crap, this is horrible. You've gotta be kidding me with that."

So when I'm done, Bob says to me, "So what do you think of the fat lady?" And I'm like, "Is that gonna be every night, you're gonna do that?" just to kind of double check that I didn't get it wrong. But he confirmed it for me. It was gonna be every show, every night.

In retrospect, I should have just said, "Wow, this is the greatest thing I have ever seen in my entire life. This is fantastic!" But I'm so bad at that, and the only thing I could come up with was, "Okay, so how much electricity does it take to power this thing?"[16]

So I do the audition, and it's a silent room. There's no audience, and Bob and that woman don't laugh at all. I guess they were busy taking

---

[16] Richie interjected at this point: "We also used the fat lady to get comics off the stage when their set was done. We had heard that the other clubs used the red light, but we were familiar with the expression, 'It ain't over till the fat lady sings.' This was more like, 'It is over when the fat lady laughs.' That's how they knew to get offstage."

notes. So anyway they're like, "Okay, thank you very much," and I left. I didn't get a call. Nobody called me to come in, and I was like, "Oh, jeez."

So I knew Larry Cobb from working at Catch, and I told him I never got a call from anyone. He said to me, "Don't worry about that, I'll get you on. We're gonna have performing times, like a real schedule, so don't worry."

And he did get me on. The Strip had a crowd because they had advertising on every bus that passed. And besides the regular spots, they would also call me on nights when I wasn't scheduled 'cause sometimes they'd run out of acts, and I lived five minutes away, in the same place I still live today. As long as there was one person in the audience they would keep the show going, so I'd be here at two in the morning in front of five people.

They'd tell me to do whatever I wanted, so I'd do a half hour at two in the morning. It was great practice for me.

I have a funny Lucien story as well. I have never drank, and the club saved a fortune on me over the years. I only drink soft drinks. I would nibble on nuts and chips and things like that, but no alcohol. So one time, the club ordered bananas for their banana dacquiris, and the bartenders would give me bananas. Lucien stopped me from having bananas. I was not allowed to eat the bananas.

So I said to him, "But I'm allowed to have a banana dacquiri right?" And he said, "As many as you like!" "But I can't have a plain banana?" "Nope!" He held a distinction between me eating a banana and ordering a banana dacquiri where they would have to use the same banana I would eat.

Lucien and I had, I don't know if you would call it a love-hate relationship, but Lucien critiqued my act till the day he died. On a weekly basis he critiqued my act, and the best part about Lucien's critiques, he wasn't shy about sharing them with the rest of the club. He'd sit out there at the bar in his booth and start talking to you about your act, like, "Well, I'm not sure if it's going well or if we're going to be able to give you any more spots here," and everybody's there. He would do this in front of everyone.

But he was great if there was a problem with a customer. I remember once when some guy either didn't want to pay, or couldn't pay, and Lucien goes over and starts talking to them and talking to them and talking to them. He was going on and on and on until finally they paid their bill, probably just to shut him up.

I think I hold the dubious record for the only comic who is still performing here at the club every night since it opened in 1976. And I've been teaching the comedy class here on Monday nights for about fifteen or sixteen years. We haven't done auditions on Monday for many years. Auditions are now on Tuesday nights after the show.

Joe Bolster

Joe Bolster is a comedian and comedy writer and is a regular on late-night talk shows and at festivals such as Just For Laughs in Montreal. He previously had a half hour special on HBO called *One Night Stand* and starred in the Comedy Central shows *Sports Monster* and *Short Attention Span Theater*.

When did you first get to The Strip, and what are some early memories?

I didn't get to The Strip until 1979. And in that year, I was working for Bill Bradley in his senatorial campaign. I grew up in Princeton, New Jersey, and my dad was the director of admissions at Princeton when Bill was a student there, so I knew him from about the age of ten on.

They had been in touch for years, and when Bill announced he was going to run for Senate, I was fresh out of college and needed a job, so I was hired as a jokewriter.

Some of my later credits are *The Tonight Show*, *Letterman*, *Conan*, and an HBO One Night Special. I'm the oldest of fourteen children, which was the foundation of my original act.

By the time I came, the performers themselves used to be the MCs, Jerry Seinfeld among them, a policy that was rife for corruption. Jerry was the MC the night I came to audition and he passed me, so that gave you entrée to hang out at the club and that would lead to you getting spots, and the spots would improve as you improved yourself.

Any funny stories?

I think so. A couple of months after I passed, I was fortunate enough to get not only one spot on Saturday night but two spots. We used to have three shows in those days, as they do now. And, as I'm sure you know, Lucien, who was an iconic figure here, was both articulate and verbose. But this was my first encounter with the Lucien that we all came to know and love.

Now on the weekend it was very important that you show up, unlike during the week when people would be hanging out who would move in like sharks to take someone's spot if they didn't show up. But on the weekend shows there were only five guys and you had to show up, 'cause if you missed your spot, it was huge, 'cause there was no one to plug in.

So here I am with two Saturday night spots, and after the first show I guess I did well, 'cause I was fortunate enough to meet a young lady after the show. Now there was a comic named Peter Bales who had an apartment that he'd let us use if we needed it. So I took her back there, and things got out of control, and I wound up missing the second show. I had only been performing here like two months, so it wasn't like I had any equity built up where I could walk in like a big shot and go, "Yeah, I didn't make the show. Give me another shot."

So I knew I had to come up with a spectacular excuse with Lucien at the front of the club, so I come in and I hear [in a perfect Lucien imitation], "So, Mr. Bolster, I couldn't help noticing you were unavailable for your scheduled spot on show number two." And I'm like, "Lucien, I'm so sorry but the most horrible thing happened. At the end of my first show, I met this girl and I took her back to Peter Bales's apartment, and at the end she had an epileptic seizure." I was that good, and without missing a beat, Lucien goes, "Petit or grand mal?"

Now, I hadn't developed the story far along enough to know. But he actually continued, "Was her tongue out and her arms flailing? Were her eyelids fluttering? Did you have to administer pressure under her thorax?" I was totally clueless, and he was questioning me like I was taking the medical boards. He was determined to find out whether I really knew what a seizure looked like, and all I said was, "Well, she finally came around, but not in time for me to make the spot."

Years later, I actually fessed up and told him I made the story up, and he said, "Ohhh, Mr. Bolster, why didn't you tell me the truth?" And I never found out who covered for me that night.

The other thing that was going on in those early years was that we had a softball team, which was endlessly amusing to us because we'd play teams like Children of a Lesser God, who had no batting skills but great signs from third base.

We were really pretty terrible. Now, since I lived in New Jersey at the time, Lucien would let me stay at his apartment on the nights prior to a softball game. Then, we'd wake up at ten o'clock and go play the game. Well, the first time this happened, the club had been open till about two or three a.m., which was common in those days 'cause that's how late people hung out.

So Lucien's locking up, and he begins some story using all kind of weird references as he was prone to do like, "Robert Lowell, the poet from Massachusetts, invented iambic pentameter once." Or, "Copernicus, who I thought was a little bit fey, remarked that the planets were not aligned properly during the medieval era." And he's continuing this all the way to his apartment across town.

So we're at the apartment, and he says to me, "You can have this bunk here. I don't know why they call it a 'bunk,'" and it was non-stop. So I get into bed, and he's standing at the foot of the bed, and he's continuing, "James Madison, of course, was instrumental in The Monroe Doctrine."[17]

At one point, I woke up and realized that I don't know how I fell asleep during his dissertation, but I had, and he hadn't noticed and was talking to a sleeping person and not in the least bit perturbed or put off by the lack of consciousness of his audience. Truth be told, I don't think he even realized. "I'll tell you something funny about Dwight Eisenhower and Dean Rusk and a cabinet that I thought was a tad too liberal during the Adlai Stevenson candidacy of 1956."

He needed you to start the conversation, but after that he could have been on his own.

Last thing I want to add is that this club fostered a familial aspect that no other club had, and it's evidenced by the fact that it's thirty-five years later and we're all still in touch and friendly and happy to see each other. A lot of that is due to Richie, who always encouraged the comics to hang out and made us feel like we had a second home here at The Strip.

---

[17] At this point in the interview, all of the comics in the room were crying with laughter, because it was such a dead-on Lucien impression.

Colin Quinn

Colin Quinn is a comedian, actor, and producer best known from his days on *SNL* (1997–2000), as the co-host of MTV's *Remote Control,* and as the host of his own show on Comedy Central, *Tough Crowd with Colin Quinn.* He was one of the very few comedians ever to star on Broadway, first in *An Irish Wake* and then in *Colin Quinn's Long Story Short.* He was rated #56 by Comedy Central in the 100 Greatest Stand-Ups of All Time.

What year did you start performing and what are your earliest memories of The Comic Strip.

I think I started performing around late 1984. I did a couple of open mics out in Brooklyn at Pip's, and Jim Mendrinos—who's really the name that comes behind everybody (me, Chris Rock, Adam Sandler)—Jim Mendrinos was like a force here at The Strip, a very quiet force to the open mic'ers, and me, him, and Chris Rock were always hanging out together.

I was doing comedy for a couple of months and then Mendrinos goes, "They're looking for a bartender at The Comic Strip. You should go and get a job there. That'll get you in." So of course I get the job, and Richie wasn't around much 'cause he was running all over the place with Eddie Murphy.

I saw him breeze in once or twice, but I didn't really get a chance to meet him because, of course, I was with Lucien every minute. But believe me when I tell you, I spent about my first six months telling everybody I was going to kill the manager of The Comic Strip if he calls me a moron one more time.

'Cause I was a bartender, and I had been a bartender for a couple of years, so I thought I was pretty good at it. But I was having trouble using an old cash register there, and he'd say something like, "A moron would understand how to use that," and I was getting so mad!

He thought I was just another guy bartending just to try and get in the club, and I never denied that, but he wouldn't let me audition until I left my position as a bartender. That was a rule at the club. You couldn't do both. So I bartended for about six months before I auditioned for Lucien. But once he saw me perform, he liked me, and then of course he loved my stuff from there on.

What do you remember about Richie in the early days?

When I left Brooklyn and moved to Manhattan, I lived in an apartment about two or three blocks away from the club. And the thing with Richie was, he came in once and a while, and the reason I remember is that he was the only one that used to tip at the bar. Well, him and George Wallace. George always left a tip also 'cause he was a classy guy. The only thing was that George used to call me Cullin: "Cullin my boy, how the heck are you?"

But I didn't mind 'cause at least he knew who I was. Nobody else, including the comedians, even knew my name.

I remember one time, we were at the Christmas party and Richie showed up, and that was like the biggest thing of all. Everybody was out of their minds. You would have thought The Beatles showed up. I remember Joe Vega said, and Scott Blakeman said the same thing, that when Richie Tienken was here, he *was* the place. It was like Rick's in Casablanca.

Don't get me wrong, without him it was still a great club, and when you killed at The Comic Strip, nobody killed like that anywhere ever, maybe because of how the room was set up or the acoustics. But the laughs just bounced off the walls. When you killed here, you would walk out thinking, "Hey, you could put *any* comedian against me. I just fuckin' rocked that room!"

Do you remember your first time onstage at The Strip?

The first time I ever did stand-up comedy, aside from a police lockup, which is a whole other story, I came to The Comic Strip with a friend of mine.

I went onstage, did an audition on a Monday night, I did great. I came offstage, and this guy Chris Blittman came up to me, I'll never forget it, and he says to me, "You're a natural." So right away I think to myself, "I'm in at this club." As soon as I think that he follows up with, "Come back in a year." And he wasn't being funny; he was serious. And I was like thinking to myself, "What? I'll be on *The Tonight Show* in a year. What's he talking about?"

The truth is, he should have said, "Come back in ten fuckin' years," really, for all I knew about stand-up. So that was my first attempt, even before I bartended here. Just one of the things that happened that led me to where I am now, sitting here bullshitting with you!

Another great story about Lucien and his bout with scleroderma . . . another time back in the late '80s, we're sitting out at the bar—Richie, me, Lucien, and Joe Vega—and Lucien says, "I'm doing a benefit for something." And Richie goes, "Oh jeez, another twenty bucks? I give twenty bucks for every goddamn thing that comes along!" And Lucien interrupts with, "Actually, it's for my disease." To which Richie, without missing a beat says, "Now I gotta give him a hundred" and peels off a hundred-dollar bill right on the spot. Even Lucien laughed at that, and Lucien did not laugh easily.

I was one of the very few that didn't have a horror story about Lucien. He said I was great, and he actually liked the Shakespearean stuff I was doing at the time, and he said I was "different." I *was* very different!

It was Larry Miller that really laid it out for me one time. I forget whether it was at the Christmas party—it was at some kind of party—when Larry told me what Richie really meant to this club.

McGowan and Wachs were fine. They were regular club owners, but Richie *was* this club. He had to move on because they all looked to him as their friend, leader, father figure, whatever . . . you know, he has this natural charisma. Nobody else who's not in comedy is funny. It's very strange to find someone who is not a comedy performer who is genuinely funny . . . someone who's as quick as comedians. It's very rare. And when you have a club owner who's like that, it takes it to a new level.

In your estimation, what made The Comic Strip different?

I'll compare it to Catch. The thing with Catch was, they would bump you at the drop of a hat. I remember 'cause every fuckin' Monday, me and Chris Rock would audition and wait on line to get on, and they'd put you on. But anybody at all would walk in from LA, and they'd just bump you. It was more run by the comics and that led to corruption of the system.

The Comic Strip was run by Richie and Lucien, so it was much more fair than the other clubs in that sense. The Strip was never as political as other places.

I understand that Richie was your manager for a while. How did that come about?

I don't remember how Richie became my manager, but one day he just was. I was the sidekick on *Remote Control,* and Ken Ober was the host. I was on that show for about two-and-a-half years.

I was a writer on *SNL* from '95 to '97, and I was a cast member from '97 to 2000. I was doing "Weekend Update." I was on with Will Ferrell, Cheri Oteri, Chris Kattan, Molly Shannon, and Darrell Hammond, who's been there longer than Lorne Michaels.

So let's sum up about The Strip.

Summing up, The Strip was the ultimate workout room. And once Lucien liked you, he'd give you the freedom to work out your shit. But he was always brutally honest. "Well sir, I don't find you to be particularly funny," he might say to some unfortunate schmuck. And the guy would say, in his own defense, "I know I'm funny." And Lucien would answer, "Yes sir, I'm sure you are." The guy would say, "I made people laugh." And Lucien would counter with, "Yes, well, there's a lot of people that

Left to right: Jeffrey Gurian, Ann Curry, Gilbert Gottfried, and Richie Tienken, taken at The Comic Strip on June 15, 2008, when Gilbert was helping Ann Curry prepare for her first and only stand-up comedy performance. This happened to be the exact day I suggested to Richie that we do this book!

Richie Tienken and his young, beautiful wife, Jeannie, at The Comic Strip Christmas party in 2011.

The original menu from The Comic Strip, circa 1976.

Jerry Seinfeld's first sign-up sheet the night he came in to audition at The Strip, June 17, 1976. Note that he was graded "Good—Definitely put on Monday 6/21"! (I think they were on to something!)

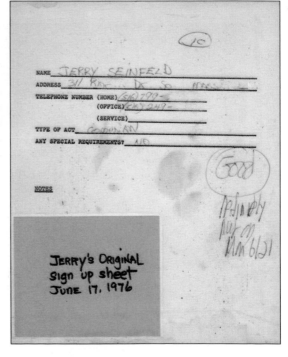

Rodney Dangerfield and Richie Tienken at The Strip in March of 1977.

Larry Miller's original headshot. He had no photos of himself, so he used a photo from a family Seder taken during Passover, and under his dress shirt he wore his Comic Strip T-shirt. This still hangs on the wall of The Strip. Photo taken around 1977.

The Comic Strip Softball Team. From left to right: Larry Miller and Bill Keller; second row (l-r): Tommy Koenig, Mark [last name unknown], Mark Schiff, Peter Bales, Steve Abrams, and unknown; third row (l-r): Hiram Kasten, [Unknown guy peeking out], Ron Richards, Jerry Seinfeld, Joe Bolster, and unknown girl; fourth row (l-r): Lucien Hold, Bob Wachs, and Kerry McNally, 1978 or '79.

A young Jerry Seinfeld on stage at The Strip, circa 1979.

A young Eddie Murphy onstage at The Comic Strip, circa '79 or '80.

Joe Piscopo and Jeffrey Gurian, while Joe was still on *SNL* and before he started working out, circa early 1980s.

Bob Wachs, Eddie Murphy, and Richie Tienken after *48 Hours*, circa 1982.

Adam Sandler, Jeannie Tienken, Richie Tienken, and a friend of Adam's, 1980s.

Dustin Hoffman and Warren Beatty at The Comic Strip during the filming of *Ishtar*, circa 1986.

A healthy Lucien Hold and Warren Beatty at The Comic Strip, circa 1986.

Steve Martin, Lorne Michaels, and Lucien Hold at The Strip, circa 1990s.

Jeffrey Gurian dancing with Gilbert Gottfried, circa 1992, from Jeffrey's "Dancing with Comedians" series.

Separate group photo taken at The Strip back in the '90s. In front: Jeffrey Ross; second row: Todd Barry and Lucien Hold; third row: Joey Vega, Chris Rock, and Mario Joyner; back row: unknown guys.

Lucien Hold and Dave Attell at The Comic Strip, early '90s.

Buddy Bolton, Adam Sandler, and Sherrod Small hangin' at The Strip, circa 1998.

Judah Friedlander, "The World Champion," accepting an award from the *Guinness Book of Records* awarded to The Comic Strip for the longest comedy show on record—50 hours—with Jeffrey Gurian, June 5, 2008.

Richie Tienken sitting in David Letterman's seat on the CBS set of *The Late Show with David Letterman*, interviewing Jeffrey Gurian as his first guest (when we went to interview Eddie Brill backstage), on August 26, 2008.

From left to right: JR Ravitz, Marina Franklin, Jeffrey Gurian, Richie Tienken, and a larger-than-life George Wallace in the back, after George did a guest spot at The Strip on September 19, 2009.

The two lions of comedy: Rick Newman, founder of Catch a Rising Star, and Richie Tienken, at The Comic Strip. Rick was Richie's inspiration for The Strip. Photo taken on February 9, 2010.

From left to right: Jordan Rock, Jeffrey Gurian, Tony Rock, Richie Tienken, and Sherrod Small (kneeling), at the Westbury Theater on Long Island for the Haiti benefit co-produced by Jeffrey, starring Kevin Hart with Tony Rock, February 20, 2010.

Jeffrey Gurian, Bob Wachs, and Richie Tienken on the Step and Repeat at the Friars Club Film Festival, for the showing of the trailer of the documentary film on The Comic Strip, 2010.

Billy Crystal and Jeffrey in Billy's offices in Beverly Hills after the interview for this book on July 11, 2011. Billy is pointing to his teeth, referencing Jeffrey's former background as "the funny dentist."

Richie Tienken, Mike Birbiglia, and Jeffrey Gurian after Mike filmed a set at The Strip for his new film featured at Sundance, *Sleepwalk with Me*, on November 9, 2011.

From left to right: Richie Tienken (seated), Rory Rosegarten, Tom Catalbiano, and Ray Romano enjoying a laugh in the tiny room where Lucien used to hold court, and which passes for an office at The Strip, 2011.

Backstage on Broadway with the cast of Chris Rock's *The Motherfu**ker with the Hat*. From left to right: Anabella Sciorra, Chris Rock, Jeffrey Gurian, Elizabeth Rodriguez, Richie Tienken, and Bobby Cannavale.

The Oldtimers, front row from left to right: D. F. Sweedler, Wayne Federman, Richie Tienken, and Joe Bolster. Back row: Bill McCarty, Jeffrey Gurian, and Ray Pasquin.

Jeffrey Gurian grabbing Richie Tienken's face in the dreaded "Jewish death squeeze," usually reserved for grandparents grabbing the faces of their poor, helpless grandchildren!

make other people laugh, but it doesn't necessarily mean that they're funny." And the guy might say, "You know what, you don't know shit." And Lucien would say, in his same tone, "Yes, okay, well, whatever you say, sir."

One time I was bartending and Lucien's mother was there. I gave her a drink, and she downs it and goes, "I'm Lucien's mother. Now you know why he's the way he is."

Talk about staying in character, Lucien would stay in character no matter what he was talking about. Even if he was talking about his dick, he'd still sound like he was in an eighteenth-century novel. Once he was talking about his first wife, Michelle. I think his best quote was, "Oh, Michelle commented on my penis . . . not so much on my size, but on my girth, which she finds satisfying apparently . . . " He would sound like Shakespeare talking about his dick. It was crazy. He was a real character.

Even The Comic Strip crowd was unique. It was always people from the boroughs, a real New York crowd, and the crowd would go insane.

Lewis Black

Lewis Black is a Grammy-winning comedian, actor, writer, playwright, and author. His "Back in Black" segment on *The Daily Show* was a long-running, highly successful segment that made Lewis a household name. He is a frequent guest on late-night TV with Conan O'Brien, Jimmy Fallon, and David Letterman. He's recorded eight CDs and has had two HBO specials: *Black on Broadway* and *Red, White, and Screwed.* His films include *Man of the Year* and Bob Saget's *Farce of the Penguins.* He's also dedicated to a variety of charity organizations.

So what year did you first start performing, and what are your earliest memories of The Comic Strip?

I don't remember! But my best guess is '89 to '90.

You first started in 1989?

No, that was when I started at The Strip. I started doing comedy around 1970. But I was doing it on and off. I didn't get serious about comedy till about 1985, 'cause that's when it kind of transitioned into more and more stand-up.

In the early days, I was talking about my sex life, which was very funny. I wasn't being me. I was trying to find a personality to bring onstage, and I didn't know how. It's that thing that like 80 percent of comics have to do except for those pricks who are instinctive. I was stumbling around, looking to bring the person who was funny when I'm offstage, onstage.

In the beginning I just did it off the cuff, and then one day I decided, "That's the problem! I'll write it all down." And when I wrote it all down, that's when I became a total piece of shit! I'd be onstage trying to tell a story I knew, but I wanted to tell it exactly the way I fuckin' wrote it!

The turning point was a guy, in about '85 to '86, a guy who was a friend of mine, Dan Ballard, who worked mainly out of the Midwest and never really did the clubs here. But he did radio and still performs to this day and is very funny. So one night here in New York at The Westbank, where even today there's a lot of Broadway and off-Broadway actors coming in to perform, I was the playwright in residence. I was doing a show with Ballard and John Bowman, who now opens for me, and Ballard comes up to me and says, "Whatsa matter with you? You know, you're up there, you're really angry, but you don't yell! I'm *not* angry and I'm screamin' all the time. You get back up there, and the next time, I don't care what you're talkin' about, I want you to yell." And that was it.

I said, "Fine," 'cause that's where my funny bone is. The anger thing wasn't the total part of my personality, but it was the part of my personality that was funny, when I was mad. So after about six months, I realized that the reason it wasn't working half the time was partly because of confidence and the rest because I'm a guy onstage sitting on my anchor! That's the creepiest fuckin' thing you can be, outside of being a pervert.

What were you doing for a living while you were meddling with comedy in the early days?

I was broke. I had studied playwriting and got my MFA in playwriting from Yale, and I'd teach a little up around New Haven. I was working in the theater mostly and doing stand-up on the side. And then when I got to New York, I started to do a little bit more, and a little bit more, and when I started running this room at The Westbank, that was the other turning point, because I was onstage every night. It's that thing about MCing. I was onstage as the host.

And how did you wind up performing in the clubs?

Well, people started hearing about me, and Rick Newman came down from Catch A Rising Star. On Saturday nights at midnight we ran a free show. There weren't a lot of comics coming in, but there were a few. And I would do stand-up every Saturday night. I'd take some newspaper clippings onstage and just go through 'em. I would just take everything that I thought was fucked up that week and talk about it onstage.

Catch was the only place I auditioned. I had just moved to New York from New Haven. This was like '78, '79. I brought three of my friends. I get in the line-up, there's like fifteen people, and I'm twelfth. There's also about twelve people in the room, including my three friends. We're all broke. I spent a hundred bucks for all of us, with two drinks and the whole fuckin' thing. I forget who the MC was, but I went up to him afterward and I asked him how I did. And he said to me, "Well, you know, everybody knows you gotta be in the first five to be auditioned." And I went into a rage. I was broke, and had just spent a hundred bucks to perform, and this guy was telling me that no one important was even going to hear me? So I picked up a chair and threw it across the room. He looked at me like I was crazy. They threw me out, and I never went back. And I never went to another club until much later.

So I leave. Rick comes to see me on occasion, but I was starting to get a name. One night he invites me to come to his club, and I said, "I'm not coming to your fuckin' club cause you fucked me!" And that was the first time I had even told him about it. He's like, "Whaddaya mean?" So I tell him the story, and he tells me it'll never happen again. He's like, "I promise. You won't have any trouble." So I call Louis Faranda, who was running the room then, and he told me not to worry, and I told him, "If you fuck me again, I'll kill you!" So I went in, and I did the gig, and it was great. And the amazing thing about that I'll never forget is that Denis Leary was onstage, and he's the first guy I see in the club. I really hadn't studied what was going on in comedy clubs.

He was doing his smoking bit, and I had a smoking bit, but his was so much better than mine, so I was like, "Okay, I just lost my smoking bit." And he was doing that smoking bit while smoking. So for about four or five months it was me, Leary, Mario Cantone, and Kevin Meaney. And then one day somebody said, "You should come down to The Comic Strip," and then I heard that Lucien wanted to see me. So then I started coming over here, and he just started putting me up.

You auditioned for Lucien?

No. He just started putting me up. I wouldn't have auditioned. Lucien really grabbed onto me. It was really terrific. It was really at the time when

I was making that transition into stand-up, and I'm broke, and I'm forty. It was really Louis Faranda and Lucien who were the two guys who gave me that confidence. Working with Lucien was like having an English professor at your house. You'd come offstage and he'd say something like, "I think if you'd say 'chatterbox' it would work better for you."

By '89, '90, I had started coming over to The Strip to work out after my own shows at The Westbank. I would do three shows at The Strip, two at Dangerfield's, and two at Catch. I could do like seven shows and make money doing that. I was like in heaven. But by the seventh show, I didn't remember what I had said.

The difference was that in this room at The Strip people paid attention to what was happening. The red light at Dangerfield's made me feel like doing heroin, which I had never done, and still have not to this day.

What do you remember about Richie in those early days?

He tried to molest me. That's the main thing I remember. He'd follow me into the bathroom, and say, "Can I touch?" and I'd say, "No, Rich!" He was a real guy, a real mensch. He actually enjoyed being there and interacting with the comics. A lot of owners are in the back room somewhere, and you never see them. Richie was always around. He was a real guy!

What about your relationship with Lucien?

To this day, I still can't understand what Lucien was doing in a comedy club. He should have been a professor at Dartmouth or the headmaster at a prep school. It made no sense. It was insane. If he had showed up one night in jodhpurs and one of those Sherlock Holmes pipes, it would have been perfect.

There were people in this business you can say are eccentric. Lucien took that to the level of, "How are you here?" eccentric. He had that musical voice thing, that lilting kind of, "Yesss, Lewis." But he was really interested in life, which was unusual for someone running a club. Usually they're interested in how they're going to save on toilet paper. But he was kind of fascinated by what you were doing in your life.

In winding down, is there anything you'd like to add about The Comic Strip?

You know, they always gave me a good drink! And you can't beat that! I have a very warm place in my heart for The Strip. It brings back memories, like, "I never got laid here!"

Billy Crystal

 Billy Crystal is an actor, writer, producer, and director who was the first comedian to set foot on the stage of The Comic Strip. He's known for his days on *SNL* and from his many films, such as *When Harry Met Sally*, *Analyze This*, and *Analyze That*. He won a Tony Award for his Broadway play *700 Sundays* and recently hosted the 2012 Academy Awards for the ninth time.

I understand that you were the very first comedian to ever hit the stage when The Comic Strip opened.

Yes, I didn't remember that until Bob Wachs called me to tell me! But I didn't know what I had for breakfast either. It was a long time ago, and Bob was my lawyer at the time.

So Bob told me he was going into the club business, and it was risky, because in New York—and this was the height of the club time and at the time of the comedy resurgence—actually, it was a *"surgence"* (it wasn't even a resurgence), there was Catch A Rising Star on the Upper East Side and The Improv of course on the West Side. Then Bob opened the place right near Catch A Rising Star, which was a dangerous thing to do because comics tend to have an allegiance to one particular club.

They tend to be very loyal to people who gave them free food or a couple of bucks for gas money, and Rick Newman of Catch was that for me. First of all, Catch was really like a hot, great room. The Improv was too far a drive for me. I lived out on The Island and I hadda get in and out of town fast 'cause I had a baby, and I hadda be up at five-thirty, six o'clock in the morning.

My wife was working, and I was a house husband with the baby, who is now a regular on the series *House*—she plays Rachel Taub, Peter Jacobson's wife—so that extra time meant a lot to me, and Rick Newman was just great to me.

Then Bob became my lawyer, and he was sort of a young, hotshot, aggressive guy, and now he's an old hotshot, passive-aggressive guy, and he asked if I would come and open his new club. And I felt kind of funny 'cause I was like a Catch act, and I didn't want Rick going, "Well I can't put you on at 11:10 tonight. How's 3:15?"

Not even in the morning! At 3:15 in the afternoon!

Yeah, just for the guys. For the guys who were vacuuming! So I did it anyway, and I remember the room. It was fun. It was like the whole room was right in front of you, as I remember. So I remember it went well, and the club took off, and I was glad 'cause it meant that the guys had another room to work out of.

So you would go up onstage at Catch every night in those early days?

Yeah, well, I was in a group first. We were called Three's Company. We had been together a long time and then we started playing Catch. It was David Hawthorne and Al Fanelli, and we were really funny, but it's hard to sell a three-man act. There had only been a couple, like Ace Trucking Company, and The Untouchables, which was Alto and Mantia and Marvin Braverman.

We were together a long time. They were my best friends, and they were very funny. But it just didn't happen, and I had a baby, and I was substitute teaching, and I was twenty-six-years-old already, and I said, "I gotta go on my own, and do this." I guess I was hiding in a group. So I told the guys I was leaving, and the next night I was at Catch. I had been writing for myself all along. Rick was great to me, and I was very prolific at that time, like this big belch of stuff came out, and in like a couple of months, I was working and was the opening act for Billy Joel, Sha-Na-Na, Melissa Manchester, and it just happened quickly that way.

How did you get your first break for something so big like opening for those big stars?

I was seen by the best managers in comedy for me: Jack Rollins, Charlie Joffe, Buddy Morra, Larry Brezner. Buddy was the one who saw me with the act, and he came to me and said, "Listen, we don't think the act is gonna go anywhere. It's really good, but it'll go just so far. But we think that you have something that we could definitely work with. Have you ever done stand-up?" And I was like, "Yeah." 'Cause I always did it when I was alone as a kid or for my brothers, but here was somebody like Buddy and Rollins telling me, "We could work with you, and we want to!"

So I said, "Okay," and then I knew I was gonna be in good hands. That's what started it, was their belief in me. I did this little fraternity party down at ZBT on Mercer Street, pouring rain, first time alone, and they all came. Rollins and Joffe, the whole office came. And I don't know how I did it. I did an hour and something, stuff just came out. It was gigantic. I was just improvising. It just came out.

And they said, "The act stinks, but you're really good. So now let's start doing material. So Buddy called Rick, and Rick was great and gave me good times, and that's how I got started.

I'm always fascinated by the synchronicity of events that cause certain things to happen in your life that change your life dramatically. Like you miss your plane and you're cursing your luck, but because you missed the plane you meet someone who becomes very important to you. Can you think of any event like that, or a lucky break that changed your life?

Well, I missed this plane . . . is it lucky? I don't know. I think hard work makes good luck. I think the situation with the guys from the Rollins-Joffe office falls into that category.

The three of us were up at the office of Buddha Records with two young producers named Lanny Lambert and Bobby Flax, and Lanny and I had gone to NYU together. They loved the act, all three of us. So we were doing an album, and we were going in and doing sessions—and it's tough without a live audience to do your stuff—and we were trying to adapt it into an album.

Eddie Sommerfeld, who used to manage Sha-Na-Na, was in the building, and he saw us and liked us, and said, "You know who's here? Buddy Morra just came in, and he's Robert Klein's manager, and they handle Cavett and they handle Woody Allen, so he should see you guys." So we basically did our whole act in a room alone for Buddy, and that started him getting us some dates and stuff.

[Author's note: At this time, I took the opportunity to remind Billy that we had actually known each other many years before.]

On a personal note, do you have any memory of meeting me a long time ago?

No. Did I?

We originally met through Jack Rollins back in the early '80s. If it spurs a memory, I was a dentist then who was also a comedy writer.

Now it's starting to come back to me. The funny dentist!

Exactly. I had written Jack a letter at the time, on my dental stationery, tell-
ing him that Woody Allen had read my material, which was true, and that
he told me it was funny and very visual and that I should consider making a
film out of it. And at the time, I had taken some short films I made up to SNL
and met Alan Zweibel [who went on to write Billy's show 700 Sundays*].*
They were very strange films, like, "Several men were arrested for smearing
cream cheese on the ankles of elderly women who wore their stockings rolled
down like bagels." And I got my own grandmother to let me put cream cheese
on her ankles for the film.

So when I met Jack, he had the idea of doing a sitcom about a dentist who
wanted to be in show business, and he thought that you would be perfect to play
me! He thought you would make a great dentist!

You know, now that we're talking, I do remember saying, "Oh, it's the
funny dentist!" I do remember that.

So back to The Comic Strip . . .

It was such an important time for me and other comics. Our group
was Richard Belzer, Jay Leno (who was an Improv guy), Richard Lewis,
Eddie Bluestone (who wrote great jokes), and the one we all looked up to
was Robert Klein.

Bob was the best comedian of that time. Really funny. David Brenner
was also very successful. *The Tonight Show* was great for him. Not only
could he come out and kill in five minutes—his material lent itself to that—
but he could also host a show, and he hosted *The Tonight Show* a lot for
Johnny. He was really good.

What kind of stuff were you talking about in those early days?

I was talking about being a young parent and about natural childbirth.
You know things happened to me earlier. I had a baby at twenty-five. And
I'd laugh 'cause ten years later guys were talking about their natural child-
birth, and I was like, "I did it ten years ago."

So even from the beginning, you never really did "joke-jokes"? Always observational humor?

Yeah. I can't write a good joke. Jack gave me the best advice I've ever gotten, and Jack knows how much I love him. It actually appeared in Marlo Thomas's book, *The Right Words at the Right Time*, about mentors and stuff and the best advice you ever got. Jack was coming in to see me. I had been out there for a couple of weeks, and I had put together a really good twenty to twenty-five minutes, and there was a lot of . . . I'm gonna use the word "routines" in them.

I was doing Ali-Cosell and kind of like "bits," and Jack came in, and I just killed. I really did great. We go out afterward, and I'm nervous, 'cause this is the guy who's gonna tell me, "I'm not gonna handle Woody anymore, it's only gonna be you!" This is what I'm thinking.

And he says, "I enjoyed tonight, but I don't think you're doing yourself any good with the kind of material you're doing." So now I'm trying to butter my toast and at the same time not stab him. And I say, "Whaddaya mean?" And he goes, "It was all funny. It was all funny, and you can do very well with this stuff and you will. But you never once told me how you felt about something. I never heard 'I' in it. Toys and games was what I heard. The audience really liked it, so take this if you want. But here's the thing: You didn't leave a tip!"

I said, "Whaddaya mean?" He said, "You didn't leave a little extra thing on the table that when you leave the waitress goes, 'That was a good guy.' You didn't let them know enough about you. They didn't go away going, 'I wanna see him again,' They got it all. But always leave a tip—that little extra thing that'll make you different than everybody else. Leave a little bit of yourself on the stage."

He went on: "Tomorrow, don't do any of this material. I don't care if you bomb for tomorrow or two weeks or three months or whatever. Start talking about *you*! Make every sentence begin with 'I think,' or,

'You know what happened to me?' and talk about real things. That's what I wanna see."

And I was just furious inside, going, "But I just killed, and they loved it," and I went home, I didn't sleep, and I got up—and I started writing. I came in the next night, and it was a little rough. But by about two weeks later, I called Jack and said, "Come take a look at this." And it didn't go as well with the audience reaction, but he said, "Now, you're really doing something." And that was really the best advice I've ever gotten.

You also did such great characters. Was it on SNL *that you developed Fernando?*

Fernando actually started on a variety show I had on NBC. We did six episodes, and it was a summer kind of thing. So Fernando started there.

The entire country was saying, "You look Mahvelous."

SNL was a perfect place for me. It was a playground. It was great! My year at *Saturday Night Live* I think is the most single-satisfying year in my career. 'Cause it set everything else off in motion. It got me into the movie world. It was like, "Hey, look what he does." And I was then thirty-six, so I was a late bloomer.

How did you know you could do characters when you come from a stand-up background?

I always did impressions. Even as a little boy I always did stuff. In my act, [Mohammed] Ali was like the first one. It was a white, Jewish kid who does him, and people went crazy for that.

Well this is a real treat for me being able to see you again after all these years.

Well, you're the funny dentist! Didn't Alan King say that to you that night they dedicated the bar to me at The Friars? Alan was there, and I remember him saying, "Don't you know him? He's the funny dentist."

A lot of people referred to me that way over the years. I was actually immortalized in the Broadway play Moon Over Broadway *with Carol Burnett, where the writer needs new jokes and Philip Bosco says, "Why don't you call the funny dentist?"*

Well, a funny guy who could do a crown is very hard to find!

CHAPTER **TWO**

THE YOUNGER KIDS

The "younger kids" are also household names in comedy. They are the younger generation of comics you see on TV and in films and listen to on the radio. Most of them are based in New York and still perform at The Comic Strip on a regular basis. The ones living in LA come and hang out at The Strip when they're in town.

Lisa Lampanelli

Lisa Lampanelli, comedy's "Lovable Queen of Mean," is not only a comedian but also an actress and an author. Her career took off quickly after her 2002 killer set on the Friars Roast of Chevy Chase. She's a regular on the Comedy Central Roasts and on *The Tonight Show with Jay Leno, Jimmy Kimmel Live, Late Show with David Letterman,* and *Chelsea Lately,* and was just on the cast of *Celebrity Apprentice.* She's had three one-hour Comedy Central specials: *Take It Like a Man, Dirty Girl,* and *Tough Love.* Lisa's also been in several films, including *The Aristocrats, Drillbit Taylor,* and has been cast in the upcoming *Sopranos* movie.

So when did you start performing comedy, and what are your earliest memories of The Comic Strip?

I started performing comedy around 1991. I thought to myself, "I'm thirty. I gotta do something else other than this bullshit journalism." I got sick of earning twelve grand a year and decided maybe I could say "cunt" for a living and make a lot of money. Luckily, that is how it worked out. And I was always into really fuckin' with the audience, because that's when I had fun, and if you're not havin' fun, they're not havin' fun. So I committed, and that's it. I have no other choice now. No going back.

I went to Syracuse undergrad and I was a journalist for like ten years. I got a job right out of college with a good newspaper in Connecticut. But they put me on a beat, so I was like covering sewer commission meetings and all this crap. So like on purpose, I plagiarized a bunch of stories because I didn't even want to go to the meetings. I'd just read the Danbury paper stories, copy them, and slightly reword them, and they caught on eventually, and were like, "You're in trouble," so I quit. So I came to New York, and I started writing for *Rolling Stone* and *Hit Parader* magazine, and I wrote about all those awful heavy metal bands.

So you were a music groupie in those days?

Not a groupie, 'cause like I was fat and didn't fuck anybody, but I actually really loved the music. But by age thirty I was like, "Okay, that was fun. My heart's not in it anymore. Now what should I do?" I decided to do comedy, and fortunately I had the nerve to try it.

So where did you start performing? What was your first comedy gig?

I took a comedy class from this guy, Michael Jackson, in New Haven, Connecticut. Not the real Michael Jackson, this guy was actually black. And he taught us how to actually put together jokes and structure the first five minutes. 'Cause you really don't know what to do the first time you go up there, and you can't just go up and wing it. So our first show was at this place Joker's Wild out in New Haven, and for some reason comedy was really big back then, so it was like full on a Tuesday night, and it was so cool.

Of all nights, Al Martin of New York Comedy Club happened to be there. I didn't know who the fuck he was, but every open mic had a headliner, so he came in and he goes, "Wow, you're good. How long you been doin' this? Do you wanna do the road?" And I was like, "That was my first time." I did like five minutes, and I do remember it went great. As a matter of fact, it went so good that the next day I called in sick, I was so uppity. I was like, "Whatever, man, no more copy editing for Lisa Lampanelli."

I never wanted to come into the New York clubs until I was a headliner, because I wanted instant respect, which worked out for me because I wasn't gonna go up any ranks. It's like, "You know what, I headlined here, here, and here." And that's how it happened.

I'd find out who was booking clubs in Long Island or New Jersey, and I figured if I could get a good ten minutes, I could MC. I was a great MC because I loved crowd work. Then I started to get the reputation—like the middle act complained 'cause he couldn't go after me—and then eventually a couple of the headliners would make fun of me from the stage 'cause they couldn't follow me, and I was like, "Fuck you, assholes."

'Cause you know I started when I was thirty, so I already had a personality. And like all those guys I call "lifers," the guys that are still headlining for like 300 bucks a night, they would get really insecure. And I was like, "Oh sorry, douchebag. I guess I'm a star, and you're not. Sorry, waaaaaah!"

I honed my act for seven years. And I started headlining really good places like Improv and stuff, on the road, and I'm finally ready to do the city. But how do I afford to live in the city? Because what I had heard was that Lucien was really hard core about comics living in the city, because he couldn't call you ten minutes before if "so and so" wasn't showing up and ask you to come in, so I wanted to be viewed that I lived here.

So what did I do? I found an elderly couple living on a sixty-acre estate ten minutes out of the city, and I cleaned their house for them four days a week in exchange for free room and board.

And that's what I tell my openers: If you haven't either slept in your car 'cause you couldn't afford the hotel room or cleaned someone's house, you're not a real comic—you're a bitch! Meanwhile, I'm putting you in The Four Seasons and you're complaining? Waaaah! Kill yourself.

So now I was ready to do the clubs, but I said, "Let me not start off with The Comic Strip, 'cause it's the one that's iconic, and the one you have to warm up to." So there was this comic Johnny Lampert, who I had met working on the road. He was like my biggest fan but also kind of a douchebag too. And he knows that too 'cause I told him.

He said to me, "Well, the minute you're ready, I'll tell Lucien to see you personally, so you don't have to go through an audition process." I said, "Absolutely, 'cause I'm not gonna do that anyway."

So how did you finally work up to seeing Lucien?

Well, this was around 1988. Carolines was starting to use me for little spots like feature spots, Catch was no longer in existence, I was doing stand-up all the time, and I decided it was time to cash in that thing with Lampert. So, I called him up and said, "Listen, man, I'm ready to audition for Lucien," 'cause at the time that was the top thing you could do in the city. So he introduced me to Lucien right there in the club, and Lucien said, "Okay, I'll see you next Monday."

Now I had heard that Lucien liked stuff that was autobiographical, so I get myself all ready, and I knew Lucien was really tough, and he'd probably make me cry. But I was like, "You know what? Fuck it, I'm so good . . . whatever!"

You have to have that ego. Ask any comic, even if he's a loser, and he'll be, "Seriously, I'm the greatest comic of all time."

So I had my little five minutes, but I'm super nervous. So I went over there and I did my audition, and then you stand there and you wait for him to pull you into that little tiny room. So, finally he calls me in and he has these notes, and he says. "Wellllllll, I see here that you do some audience work (which I didn't do much of that night), some autobiographical material with some blue asides . . ." Like he used such smart words, and he shakes his head like in distaste, and I go, all excited, "Thank you." And he goes, "What?" And I say, "Thank you. That is what I do. Very accurate description." I played it off like everything was a compliment, and he was like, "Okay." Then he stammered, "Welllll, uhhh, I don't know, you're obviously capable, and I need acts like this on the weekend, but why should I have you work here?" And I go, "Listen man, honestly. . ." and I mean this, this is how sick I am, ". . . you don't understand how much people love me. Audiences wanna see me again and again and again. I don't know what it is. It's one of the intangible qualities that I have." I said, "I'm like Sinatra." I'm that conceited, right? I went on: "It's a quality that only few are born with, and I feel that I would be an asset to this club, but obviously it's up to you. Whatever you decide is fine with me . . . whatever, man!"

So I'm in there for about an hour, and I'm not begging my case, but I'm just saying what I think about myself, telling him how good I think I am, and finally he says, "Okay, well, we'll give you a try. Call in your avails." And I still have that fucking business card he gave me. He gave me that business card with The Comic Strip name on it, and I wrote down something like, "What hours do I call?" And he was like, "Ask the girl out there." So I went out, and I asked the girl, and I was so happy, and I wrote down the hours on that card, and I called in my avails every Tuesday, I think, or maybe it was Monday. I still have that card somewhere at home.

Lucien had a gift 'cause he really knew so much about comedy. The night Lucien passed me was one of the biggest nights of my life. Honestly, in the list of "firsts," it was a huge deal, to pass on your first try, like your first *Tonight Show*, your first *Howard Stern* show.

So, I remember I called in my avails, but I was away the following week working in Florida, and I was all sad, thinking he was gonna forget me by next week. But he didn't. And I remember once he gave me eight spots in one week because there were tons of prom shows, and I always did good at those, and those were all weekend spots. But then of course, because I'm never satisfied, I said to him, "Dude, c'mon, you have to give me some weekday spots," 'cause industry used to come on weekdays. I'm never happy. I always have to want something else.

Did you do the same kind of insult humor that you do now in those early days?

Well, I didn't do it for the audition with Lucien, because he didn't want to see that. I did biographical stuff, about my life and about weight and being married. The only insults were like asides to the audience that he mentioned. I realized that once I got passed I could do whatever I wanted. It's like once you go to Harvard, you can do what you want!

Once I started, I was primarily a weekend and prom comic, and on the weekends he didn't care what I did because he needed killer shit. And sometimes even during the week, if things were a little quiet, he'd say, "Lampanelli, go wake 'em up!" And I wasn't even on the schedule. 'Cause I'm fucking good. I was like the Sparky Lyle of comedy, the pinch hitter.

Lucien's respect meant a lot to me. To me, Lucien, Howard Stern, Rickles, those were the people whose respect I wanted, and fortunately I got it. I don't know what you do if you don't get their respect, but I'm glad I got it.

I didn't really hang out if I didn't have a spot. I made sure I wasn't that person that just hung by the bar, because you always have to give the illusion that you had to be someplace else. I was so insecure; I needed to know like I had eight spots all the time. I wasn't gonna just hang out hoping he'd need me for something. I'm not your nigga! Why would I hang out, just so I could talk to these bitter douchebags? They're all so negative. I'm like, "Whatever!" So I just never did that.

Who were some of the people performing in those days?

Well, Richie was hanging out with Tony Rock in those days. We kind of came up together. Then there was Sherrod [Small], Chris Rock's cousin, D. C. Benny, Ben Bailey, Ross Bennett, who's the funniest fuck. Not a lot of chicks, which was great, 'cause they're not funny. Honestly, kill me now. There was Jim Norton, Colin Quinn, Jim Florentine, Attell . . . Attell did the funniest line about me once. He was onstage and said, "If you're looking for Lampanelli, she's outside whipping a black guy with a Don Rickles album." I always love when they say stuff about me.

Where did your first big break come from?

Oh my God, my first thing, I will always thank The Friars Club 'cause they pushed me onto that Comedy Central Roast for Chevy Chase. They would not stop harassing Comedy Central because Comedy Central didn't know me. But man, they pushed and pushed, got me on, and ever since then I got the right manager, the right agents, and *boom*, it was The Friars Club that started it all.

Any closing thoughts on The Comic Strip?

The main thing, honest to God, and this may sound corny, but one of the most important things I got from being at The Strip was the general self-esteem that you are part of this elite group of people who get to go up on that stage. 'Cause even after I passed there, I didn't have the balls to walk in unless I had spots. I remember one Saturday night coming home from some gig on the weekend, and I drove past there, and I thought, "Well I could stop over there because I am passed at the club, but should I really?" I was too insecure to even walk in.

But once I got used to the idea that I got passed at The Comic Strip, I got lots of self-esteem. It was really very powerful for me. I just felt like, "Now I can do anything." It just told me that, "Wow, I'm okay." And also, I met my first black guy that I ever had sex with at The Comic Strip. I wrote about it in my one-woman show, "Chocolate Please." So I think I should thank Lucien for that.

In the beginning, I dressed like such a fat dyke. I had really short dyed red hair, really dykey clothes. 'Cause you know when you're overweight, you feel, "I might as well not even try." But Lucien always gave me mad respect. It was really cool. Thank God I have enough ass left for the blacks. But now I can go either way. Lisa Lampanelli, not just for blacks anymore![18]

Last thing. Do you remember, back before your career kicked in, when you and I were going to start a Roast business together? We even had brochures planned out and everything.

Yeah, yeah, yeah. Of course I remember. We were gonna do corporate roasts. I always wanted to find new ways to make money.

Yeah, and right before we started, like two weeks later, your career took off, and we never did it.

Ahhh, poor Jeffrey. You're doing fine. I see that car you're driving. Don't worry about it!

---

[18] Since this interview, Lisa married Jimmy Canizzaro, a white guy she affectionately refers to as Jimmy "Big Balls"!

Jim Breuer

Jim Breuer is a comedian, actor, radio personality, and author. Jim rose to fame as a cast member of *SNL* from 1995 to 1998. He had two one-hour Comedy Central specials, the second one being one of the highest-rated specials in Comedy Central history. A frequent guest on *Opie and Anthony*, he had his own radio show, *Breuer Unleashed,* which is now called *Fridays with Breuer* on Sirius radio. Jim has been in numerous films, including *Half Baked, Beer League,* and *Zookeeper.*

What year did you start performing comedy, and what are your earliest memories of The Comic Strip?

The exact date was 1985. I was just finishing high school, and a girl who was anorexic lived across the street from me. Now I had already performed out in Long Island at a place called Governeurs. But this anorexic girl called me from the hospital, and she said to me, "There's a man here in the hospital with me who says he runs this comedy club in New York called The Comic Strip, and his name is Lucien, and I'm gonna talk to him about you."

So she did, and she gave me the address of the club, and I finally went in and went to the club and found out I had to fill out like a lottery thing to get a spot to perform, and I guess it was my lucky night because my number got picked. A lot of the other guys were jealous, I remember.

So I think it was a Tuesday night, and in my head I'm remembering Eddie Murphy's album *Delirious,* which was made at The Comic Strip, and I'm thinking that from the moment I go onstage, I'll be the white Eddie Murphy. Tonight I'm gonna be discovered.

So when I walk into The Comic Strip, Lucien says to me, "You go on in fifteen minutes," and I was petrified. I went to look in the room, and there was nobody there. When I played out on Long Island, I packed the place with my friends and my family, so this was gonna be the first "there's nobody in here" performance, but this is one of the reasons I'll never forget my first time there.

There was a black kid onstage, and what was great was he was about my age, like about seventeen or eighteen years old, and he's got this funky haircut, and he's talking to this birthday party, and there was a balloon there for the party, and there's hardly anyone there, and he goes into this bit about the Huxtables [in Chris Rock's voice]: "What kind of a show is this about a black doctor? I'm black, and I ain't never seen a black doctor married to a black female lawyer." And I went, "Oh my God, this kid is so freakin' funny." And when he came offstage, I remember saying to him, "Hi, I'm Jim Breuer, I'm a comedian." And he was like, "Oh yeah, Chris . . . Chris Rock," and I couldn't get him out of my mind. That's the kind of impression he made on me. I would always look for him.

Then about a year or two later, I would see him on like a comedy special, and then I saw him in *Beverly Hills Cop*. I remember seeing him on a comedy special and getting all excited and yelling out, "That's the kid! That's the kid that I saw." And so he was the very first guy I ever saw at The Comic Strip and I had to follow him, my very first time onstage at this club. It wasn't a pleasant evening after that. I don't remember exactly how I did. I just know it wasn't good, because I wasn't asked to come back.

And I would have had to draw the lottery again, and I knew I wasn't gonna do that. The truth is, I didn't deserve to be passed that night. I really wasn't ready.

Then I moved to Florida for a while and worked a lot down South, but I moved back to New York on the promise from some big comedy manager that he would represent me. I had spent a whole year working hard, like triple shifts and saving all my money to do that, and when I got here, he changed his mind and said he couldn't represent me. He used to drop Eddie Murphy's name a lot and told me he'd get me on MTV and VH1. It was devastating, but it actually worked to my advantage 'cause it made me work harder, and then everyone wanted to represent me.

It wasn't until I got on TV with Uptown Comedy Club, where I was the token white guy, that I had the confidence to try the New York clubs again. And I tried the downtown clubs, but it was The Comic Strip by far where I felt the most comfortable, where I felt the best audiences were, and I ripped that place to shreds.

And I remember I constantly would have to follow Ray Romano. One time, I remember, Ray comes in and crushes the place. This was before he got *Raymond*. And I had this big development deal going on at NBC, and I'm waiting for Ray to come off so I can tell him. So I go, "Ray, I have this sitcom in the works, and you know it's a young married guy, and I think you should be the head writer, you got great marriage material." And he goes, "Well, I, uhhh, I kinda got my own deal going on." And I'm like, kind of sarcastic and all, "Yeah, well, let me know how that works out for ya! Mine's gonna be a monster!"

Once I started working the rooms in the city, that's when I started realizing my potential. I would absolutely *crush* at The Comic Strip. That was my favorite place to work out. This club was my city home and will always be my city home.

What do you think made The Comic Strip so special?

There was just an electricity there for me. The crowds were great. They came there to laugh. You know, it was Richie who helped me figure out that I look high all the time. I'd go out onstage and the audience would start giggling before I even said anything, and I never really understood why. They were laughing at the way I looked, and one night Richie said to me, "You know, you look wasted." I have the kind of eyes that make me look perpetually stoned. So I went out there and said, "By the way, I'm not high." And the audience roared, and that became the beginning of my opening forever after that.

So did you ever actually get passed by Lucien?

I tested for him eventually, and this time I passed immediately. I was doing Harlem clubs—The Apollo, The Uptown Comedy Club—I did some downtown clubs, but I *really* wanted to do The Comic Strip, because that was the first club I had gone into and I hadn't done that well. So it was important to me on many levels to go back and be accepted there.

So I went there, and I wrecked the place. I totally destroyed. It was like I brought in a demolition crew. Lucien was like, [in Lucien's voice] "Yes . . . well, you know, you're certainly TV material, and I just love your energy . . ." and I remember that because no one had ever commented on my energy before. "It was fantastic, and I really think Richie is going to enjoy seeing you here." And that's how I got back here. It was phenomenal.

And even in my *Saturday Night Live* days, I would only work here. I had a manager who had downtown clubs; I wouldn't go there. I only wanted to work The Strip. I didn't need the money, and downtown just wasn't home. This was home for me.

So who were some of the comics you came up with in those days at The Strip?

Well Ray [Romano] would be there. Then there was Jon Stewart once in a while. Chris Rock would pop in to work out. Me and Chris had a really weird thing happen at The Comic Strip, which as a matter of fact I brought up to him recently, and Chris said [in an excellent Chris Rock impersonation], "Oh yeah, that was my Corvette days. That was my Corvette, I'm a dick stage."

That night that this occurred, I got really upset with him. What happened was, I was onstage working something out, and at the time I was on *SNL*. I had also just started doing MTV *Beachhouse*, which really turned out well for me and gave me a lot of recognition. So, I'm onstage at The Strip, and as soon as I got off, Chris went up. But when he was up there, he must have remembered that one time his company called me and asked me if I would come in and do a sketch on his HBO show. I said I'd love to, so they sent me a date and of all times it was the date of my family reunion. I was like, "Ohhhhh man, of all days." So I told them, "I'd love to be on your show. Can I possibly come on any other time?" And I didn't hear from them again. I never heard back on anything.

So this was the first time I had seen him since that incident. And Chris yells out to me from the stage, "Hey, Jim, you know we called you." And I said, "Yeah, I know. Thank you, but I couldn't do it. I had to attend a family reunion." And then he said, "You know, you're supposed to do MTV and then *Saturday Night Live*, not *Saturday Night Live* and then MTV." So I yelled back, "Oh, I didn't know you were managing me." I was so pissed at him. Mostly because he went onstage and talked down to me in front of the audience. It would have been different if he had said it in private, but to do it onstage it wasn't right.

What made it hurt more was that he was the first guy that ever gave me hope when I first came in to The Comic Strip. But when he came on my radio show recently, and I brought it up to him, he was like, "Man, I'm sorry. I went through a phase where I pissed off a lot of people." So that was cool. I finally got closure, and now I'm his biggest fan again. But to be honest with you, I was already!

Any other stories you'd like to share?

I used to hang out here every night with Richie at the bar, and I'd never drink. I was never a party comic. I didn't get wasted or drink or smoke pot. My wife was there with me when we had nothing, driving the Ford Escort. We'd drive in from Long Island, and she'd park outside The Comic Strip. She very rarely came in to see me work. She'd just sit and wait in the car for me to finish, so we didn't have to spend money on parking.

Pete Correale

Pete Correale was named by *Entertainment Weekly* as one of the top ten comics to watch. His first Comedy Central special was *The Things We Do For Love*. Pete has had numerous appearances on *The Tonight Show with Jay Leno, Late Night with David Letterman*, and *Last Call with Carson Daly*. He co-hosted the Sirius satellite radio show *Breuer Unleashed* for four years with Jim Breuer.

So when did you start performing, and what are some of your earliest memories about The Strip?

I started performing around late '94, and the first place I started wasn't The Strip. I grew up around here, and I was a late bloomer to stand-up. I always watched stand-up with my brother, but I always saw it as this kind of unattainable thing that we couldn't do.

I grew up on Long Island, my father was an architect, my mother was a school teacher. People like us don't do comedy. We go to college and get a degree. So that's what I did. When I graduated, I was working the front desk at a hotel in Manhattan, and I walked by The Strip every single day.

I would look through the glass and see who was playing on the monitor, but I still never thought I could do it.

When I finally decided to try it, I was at Hamburger Harry's, and then I got a job mopping and sweeping the floors at New York Comedy Club, which no disrespect to that place but it's kind of a dumpy room. However, it's a great room when your material stinks to get better in. And guys would come in there and say, "We won't even try to go to The Strip until we're ready, because Lucien will get a bad impression of us if we go too soon."

So finally, after a year of performing stand-up every night and working a day job in the Southgate Tower Hotel, directly across from Madison Square Garden, from seven in the morning till three in the afternoon, I'd go home, take a quick nap, go to the club, clean and mop before the show, hang out all night, go on last in front of two people, get home by one, take a nap, and do the same thing all over again the next day. I'd sleep twice in a day, but I did what I had to do. So finally, after a year of doing this, comics started telling me, "You gotta go up to The Strip, you gotta hit The Strip." They thought I was ready.

So finally I'm gonna come by for an audition, and as it happens, Jim Breuer stops in, which is how I actually met Breuer, and I'll never forget this till the day I die. I'm sitting up here in the back section of The Strip, and I'm waiting to go on, and I'm so nervous, and its getting later and later, and I've been performing for about a year, and I see Jim in this little booth area with his wife, Dee, and I didn't really even know who he was. He's giggling and talking with his wife, and it's at least 11:30, and it's kind of quiet in the club, and they tell me that Breuer is going on next and not me. I'm like, "Ohh, this guy, c'mon!" But I said that to myself.

So Breuer goes on, and I'll never forget, because I never saw anything like it. First of all, he's standing with his heels on the base of the mic stand, and the mic stand is running up his back, and he's sort of balancing on it.

I never saw anything like it in my life. He's just hanging out like he's in his living room . . . if he happened to have had a mic stand there.

When I was out onstage, I lit one cigarette after the next to the point where the crowd would actually say to me, "Another one?" So for me to see someone come out onstage so relaxed was an amazing experience for me. He had just gotten back from Great Adventure, where after the water ride you can stand on the bridge and water squirts all over you and shit. Anyone who's ever been to Great Adventure knows that . . . as a matter of fact, his wife was still wet.

Now first of all, who goes to an amusement park and then comes and does stand-up? Before I perform, I need to nap, I need to rest, I need to get ready and learn my jokes. I never saw a guy like this who gets up there and he was doing fifteen minutes on his trip to Great Adventure, and it was better than anything I had ever done at the time. And he was just making it up as he went.

Then he did this thing on ice cream, it gets this huge laugh, he says, "Wow, that was good." He pulls out his pad, says, "Excuse me," and writes it down while he's up onstage. I'm thinking, "Man, he's breaking all the rules."

And then there's a guy laughing so hard he fell off his stool. I guess he had been drinking too much, and Breuer looks at him and goes, "Hammer, you all right man? Get up, get up." And that was another side of Breuer. He didn't make fun of the guy. He made it seem like it was okay to fall. Most comics would have totally embarrassed the guy, like, "What, are you a wasted idiot?" But he made the guy feel okay about it.

So Breuer winds up doing forty-five minutes, if not an hour, to the point where they tell me I should come back another time 'cause it just wouldn't be fair, and they were gonna close it out, which I was cool with, and he came off, and I didn't really meet him that night 'cause he left kind of quickly.

It probably took me another three or four months before I got an audition here, but I got so much more out of watching him that night than I ever would have gotten out of going onstage. It just changed my outlook on the whole thing about performing.

And what happened when you finally got the audition?

Right before I had gotten a real audition here someone had recommended me, and they threw me up late one night, and no one from the club was even watching, or so I thought, and afterward it was good, and I said my goodnights, and I literally got halfway down the block, and "Mad Dog" Madigan, who was bartending then, yells out, "Hey, Pete!" I'm like, "What's up?" and I go all the way back, and he says, "You're really funny man. You got some good stuff. You should come back. I want you to come back, and have Lucien see you." And that was also so important for me. I'll never forget it. I called my father all excited and went, "Dad, the bartender at The Comic Strip just came up to me and liked what I did and told me to come back to see the other guy. That's more important, Dad, than anything, cause the bartenders see everybody. They see *everybody*."

And it's those little things that mean so much. That is etched in my mind more than when I did *The Tonight Show*, 'cause those little things matter more when you're first coming up.

The thing about Jimmy and this club is that when we're on the radio, not only does he bring this club up all the time—"This is the place, this is the place!"—when I finally did get friendly with him and told him about seeing him perform that night, he said to me, "You know, you can't keep playing 'B rooms' and expect to get good. You gotta go to The Strip." Just the aura of this place is so amazing. Like in the other room there's a headshot signed by Jerry Seinfeld that says, "To the only club I ever played that at one time was the only club I ever played!" I'm like, "Even what he writes on a headshot is clever and hilarious. That guy doesn't do anything unless it's gonna be funny."

The last thing I want to say is about Lucien. I finally got a chance to audition for Lucien, and of course I thought he'd say to me, "Wow, you're great." Every comic thinks that. So I go and do my set, and I'm sitting with him in the back, and I'm so damn nervous cause this guy is like an icon . . . like Lucien Hold, he was *it!*

And everyone thought he owned the club. I got here way after Eddie Murphy and those years, but one time I came with Breuer, and Richie was here, and Breuer says to me, "C'mon, I'll introduce you to the owner." And I'm like, "What are you talking about, I know Lucien." And he's like, "Lucien runs it. You gotta know Richie, man. This is the Godfather." I was shocked. I'm like, "Lucien's the front man for another guy? I didn't even know it went past Lucien." To me, it was like Lucien, Lorne Michaels, Letterman—it goes from Lucien to them.

So I do my set, Lucien brings me in the back office, and he goes, "You seem to have a very blue-collar act up there. I'm assuming your family is blue collar?"

And I agreed. I went, "Yes, yes they are."

He's like, "What does your father do?"

I'm like, "He's an architect, and he actually just became a partner in the firm." "And your mother?" "She's a school teacher." He goes, "Not very blue collar at all, are they?" I'm like, "Well, my uncle's a steamfitter," and I'm thinking to myself, "What the fuck does this have to do with anything? My parents ain't comin' in." But I was so god-damn nervous, you know. And then by the end of it he was like, "You have a lot of natural ability. You just need to get a little polish on your jokes."

The biggest thing was, I knew I had a lot of personality, and I wasn't afraid to be up there. But he made me realize I needed more jokes. I used to call it "the Sunday night set." When you play a place all week, you can get by from Wednesday to Saturday with a couple of ideas and a good crowd. But when Sunday comes around, you're tired of dancin', and you wanna have good enough jokes where you can just stand up there and say them half asleep, and they'll still kill. And I didn't have that, and that's what Lucien wanted me to go get.

By around the year 2000, I was playing The Strip whenever I wanted. Since I've started doing the radio, I've been doing The Strip more and more. One of the things I'm so grateful to The Strip for is that I got an hour Comedy Central special coming out that I feel really good about. And the number one reason that I feel good about it is because of JR [Josh Ravitz, manager of The Strip] and this man here, Richie Tienken, 'cause nothing happens here without Richie's okay.

So with a month to go to my special, I thought to myself, "You gotta work an hour every night." But I can't dilly dally with a fifteen-minute spot here and there, so JR sends me an email asking for my avails, and I send back one saying, "The next month, I'm only doing an hour, so I'm trying to play out on The Island, or The Stress Factory in Jersey, or wherever I can get that much time onstage. I appreciate you getting in touch, but I'll hook up with you next month after I finish taping the special."

The very next day, I see an email from JR. I'm like to my wife, "What happened? This guy didn't read my email?" And then I open it up and I have seventeen one-hour spots over the next month, all for myself. I almost cried. I had goose bumps. I literally got choked up to my wife. I'm like, "Baby, I can walk ten blocks and work this out at the best club."

And they just emailed me yesterday with a rough cut of the special, and it looks great, and they're like, "Tell us who you want in the credits." I'm like, "Richie Tienken, JR, and the club, 'cause I couldn't have done it without them." Who else am I gonna thank, my dad? I don't know.

Adam Ferrara

Adam Ferrara is a comedian and actor who starred as Chief "Needles" Nelson on Denis Leary's hit FX show, *Rescue Me*. He is the host of the History Channel's *Top Gear*. He's appeared in movies such as *Mall Cop* and has been a regular on the TV shows *The King of Queens*, *Ugly Betty*, *Law & Order*, and *The Job*. He's garnered two American Comedy Awards nominations for Best Stand-Up and had three Comedy Central specials.

When did you start performing comedy, and what are your earliest memories of The Comic Strip?

July 13, 1988, was my first time onstage, and my first memory of The Comic Strip happened long before I actually got there because I was a Long Island comic first. I started out at East Side Comedy with Rich Minervini, which is now an Italian restaurant, and Governeurs out in Levittown, and Jimmy's Comedy Alley in Queens, which isn't there anymore. But the city was always the place you wanted to go to. It was like *Saturday Night Fever* [at which point Adam went into a hoarse Brooklyn Tony Manero kind of voice]: "We gotta get across the fuckin' bridge."

But you didn't wanna go before you were ready, so I was still working on Long Island, and the city was still this mythical place that you never quite felt ready for. And then Eddie Murphy's album came out, and it was taped right here in the club. I still have that album, plus all those other vinyl comedy albums: Carlin, Robert Klein, Mel Brooks' *Two Thousand Year Old Man*, Richard Pryor. I used to keep them under my bed along with the *Sports Illustrated* issue with Cheryl Tiegs in that mesh outfit. I figured that was all the stuff I'd need to survive in case the bomb went off. I didn't really know what I wanted to be, but comedy had just started coming on TV. It was before the glut of comedy shows, and the first thing I remember seeing was Pryor. We went to one of those parties your parents bring you to on a Saturday where you get the warning in the car, when your mom leans over and says, "Now you're gonna behave yourself, you hear me? Your father does business with these people."

All the adults were watching Pryor, and of course the kids couldn't watch. Then the adults left to have coffee, so of course I snuck in, and being Italian and therefore genetically handy, I figured out how to work the VCR and watched Pryor's Santa Monica concert, and it just was like . . . *boom!* I didn't understand a lot of it, but I remember thinking, "He's just talking, but look what he can do!" And that's what did it for me.

The first time I went onstage, I made the mistake of telling my mother what I was doing. My entire neighborhood shows up, so if I'm not funny, I can't leave my house.

But I did well, and the next day I went down to see my father at work, and he looked at me with pride, and I'll never forget that look, because he never looked at me like that before, and I knew then that comedy was what I wanted to do.

I felt comfortable onstage and I felt that I belonged there. Anyone can be funny on Thanksgiving, but it's another thing to be funny when there's a two-drink minimum. Try and be funny on a Tuesday night! That's how you know you can be funny!

So tell me how you finally made the transition from working on the Island to coming into Manhattan, and how did you wind up at The Strip?

Well, first I came in and just watched. I didn't want to perform. I just wanted to observe, and I always took souvenirs in those days. Prom night was a big thing in those days, and when you came out for prom night, you'd go to a comedy club. So we went to The Strip for our prom. I came in and looked around, and I took everything I could get my hands on. I took those little table-tents that advertised what acts were coming up, and I took napkins that said Comic Strip just to try and kind of absorb it all. I had no idea I was ever coming back.

I figured out pretty early in the evening, I'm not getting laid. I put that together at the dance, so I just decided to enjoy the comedy. I loved the show, and I just continued watching and watching before I ever got onstage in the city.

The first time I actually got onstage in Manhattan was at Stand-Up New York. When I first came to The Comic Strip, I didn't pass. Lucien took me into the little room and gave me "the long stare" . . . you know that look that Lucien used to use? Then finally he said, "You know you're very personable. You're very funny. But I don't need another white comic." And I'm sitting there going, "Okay, skin grafts is out." How do you answer that statement? I'm like, "Please take me. I'm not that white." What are you gonna say? "It's just the lighting?"

Then he said, "You know, I saw your tape, and you did the same material on the tape as you did here."

So now I'm thinking to myself, "Okay, that was my best stuff on the tape, and I wanted to do my best stuff for Lucien. I can't change my skin color, but I can change my material." So I started writing more with plans to come back. So, in effect, it was a good thing that he didn't pass me because it inspired me to write new stuff.

I went back to Long Island and went into my comedy laboratory, created some new stuff, played around with it for a while, and came back again. And again I saw Lucien and again he said, "Very funny. Still white. Thank you very much."

Then I got on TV and got a TV credit, and I thought that would help, but it didn't. I had done MTV, and Caroline's *Comedy Hour*, 'cause you have to remember that in those days everyone had a stand-up show.

I actually taped a VH1 thing here at The Strip, and I remember seeing Lucien and I said to him, "I know I'm still white, but I am onstage and I'm even on TV. Anything?" And I got nothing. Unfortunately, there was no affirmative action for white Long Island comics. There were no quotas that anyone needed to fill. Nothing. And then I came back one more time, and then he passed me.

I was already playing on TV, and it took him five times to pass me. He never even actually gave me the satisfaction of using the words "you passed." He just told me to start calling in for spots, but that was good enough for me.

And then, wouldn't you know, right after I passed I got a deal and moved to LA. All that effort to get accepted at The Strip, and then I leave town. I got a deal for a pilot named *Adam*, and I was so naïve at the time, I didn't even realize what an accomplishment that was, to actually get a pilot made.

What made you leave LA?

First of all, I was out there for seven pilots. That's how you tell time in LA. Seven pilot seasons had come and gone, and then I got the opportunity to test for *The Job*, the cop show with Denis Leary. I got the job on *The Job*, we shot in New York, so I moved back here. And I couldn't go out on the road 'cause we were shooting. That gave me an opportunity to work at The Strip again.

I always feel you can be a better comic in New York. Two reasons for that: one is more stage time, and they're real people in the audience. There's no industry here per se. You can get an audience of real, regular people, which is important to a comic.

LA is a factory town. Show business is the product and everyone's connected to it, so even if you're up onstage and you're good, people are gonna sit there, and not laugh. They're gonna go, "That's funny! That's really funny! I'm hysterical," without even cracking a smile. No one laughs out there.

When I would write stuff out of town and come back into New York to work it out, it was like you go out and get your cocaine, then you come home to the city clubs and you boil it down and you make crack out of it. And you always edit it in New York. You can get away with a lot of shit in Milwaukee that you can't get away with in New York. New York forces you to be the best you can be. It's either funny or it's not.

Sherrod Small[19]

Sherrod Small is a comedian and television personality who headlines venues across the country. He is a regular on VH1's *Best Week Ever*, as well as Fox News's *Red Eye with Greg Gutfeld*.

What year did you start performing, and what are some of your earliest memories of The Comic Strip?

When I first started performing was like 1998, but my first memories of The Comic Strip were way before that, when we used to come here with Chrissy [his name for Chris Rock]. That was a hot year for me, 1998. We

---

19 The funny thing about Sherrod's interview was that he spoke in "we" instead of "I." Everything he talked about was "we" did this, and "we" did that. "We" included him and his cousin—and Chris Rock's brother—Tony Rock. Sherrod spoke like they were Siamese twins joined at the sense of humor, which is so interesting because it was very rare that he would say, "When I came offstage." It was always, "When we got offstage." Yet, he performed alone. That's how closely he relates to Tony Rock.

already looked at The Strip like it was an iconic place because of Chrissy and him sleepin' outside the place and comin' up here performin'. He would come up here early and sleep in his dumb little red Toyota outside the buildin' and wait for his spots. Even if he didn't have spots, he'd sleep in front of the buildin', wait to see if somebody cancelled, and then do his spot and drive back to Brooklyn. In the heart of Bed-Stuy. You never been there in your life, Jeffrey!

So tell me about the early days.

Well, when Chrissy first started performing we were like ten, eleven, twelve, or so. Really young, and by "we" I mean me and Tony Rock, Chris's brother. But he'd come back after performing and tell us all the stories, and what was goin' on, and he'd write his jokes and test them out on us in the house before they came out, and we'd try and add our little tidbits to it. It was really fun.

So from hearing him talk about The Comic Strip, I knew that some day I wanted to perform there. We always copied what Chrissy did anyway. So we knew that whatever he did, we would do something close to that. Me and Tony started comedy the same day in July of 1998. The first show we ever did was like a little bringer show at The Boston Comedy Club, and the very next day we were at The Comic Strip. It wasn't even an audition night on a Monday when we came. Before we even did Monday, we did rehearsal shows before we went up to get passed here. 'Cause you don't wanna go straight to the Lotto, like straight to the Monday show, and then not get accepted. So we actually tried to hone some talent before we tried to be accepted.

So who did you audition for when you came here? Was Lucien here at the time?

Lucien was here every day, but Richie gave these two girls, Jeannie and Mariel, their own show, which was the only way they'd get onstage.

They worked here during the day, answering phones and stuff, and we auditioned for them first to be part of their show. Working here makes you addicted to comedy.

I remember that Colin Quinn was a bartender here when he first started, right? And he was skinny then too, wasn't he? I remember meeting Colin when Chris brought him out to Brooklyn. He was the only white guy who had the nerve to come on the block who wasn't the mailman.

So let me get this straight. You and Tony decide you're gonna do comedy, so you do one show at Boston Comedy Club, and then go right to The Strip? What made these girls let you onstage? Was it an open mic?

Well, we had done some little open mic things like at a grocery store, an actual grocery store on 7th Avenue. Like a real grocery store, you know, like aisle 2 potato chips, and we had a portable mic. And I think they may have seen us there. Probably while they were shopping. We also performed in a laundromat with Jodi Wasserman and Danny Cohen in a little show we called *Spin Cycle* in a laundromat also on 7th Avenue and 27th Street. It was even covered on New York 1 one time.

So what was your first time like at The Strip? Do you remember your first time onstage?

The first time onstage that Richie watched us it was packed in here for some reason. Absolutely packed. It was one of those Wednesday or Thursday shows, and he came down to watch us to see if we could go on one of those Monday shows, so we were already nervous, but we were ready to do it. We were so hungry for it that we damn near slept in here.

Me and Tony would join acting classes just to meet new people: "Hey, good to meet you, and as a matter of fact, I just happen to have a show tonight." That's how we'd get three or four new people to come to the show. I had acting class about four, it would end around seven, and then we'd head up here and sleep in the back of the room until the show would start. We didn't even have a car to sleep in out front like Chrissy did. We had to sleep in the building. We did a lot of things in that back area, but that's for the next book. So anyway, Jeannie and Mariel had told Richie about us and asked him to come and see us.

It was like magic that night, and I didn't want to get off that fuckin' stage. I don't know if it was the crowd, or what, but there was something in the air. It was a Wednesday night show that felt like a Saturday night show, and it just seemed like every joke smashed. I remember like Jeannie and Mariel. When we came off, they were like crying in the green room. They had tears in their eyes from laughing so hard, and they knew it was a special moment. They were really proud of us 'cause they knew that Richie and Lucien were watching.

So when I got off, Lucien spoke to me in the famous booth here, and he was like, "Great set," and I still felt like I was onstage. And Tone hadn't gone on yet. He was going on right after me, and he killed also, and when he came offstage we hugged, and we went outside and cried like two babies. We walked out of here calm, walked to the corner of like 82nd Street, and just cried like two babies.

What was your relationship to Lucien? Everyone has a Lucien story.

Lucien was an odd character. There'll never be another Lucien. I loved Lucien, but he struck fear into comics. They all walked around so scared of him. But me and Tone were like oblivious to it, 'cause we looked at him like Uncle Lucien. So we would be jumpin' around makin' noise, and we would see him givin' somebody shit, and they'd look at us and say, "Why don't you give them shit?" And he'd just say, "Ahhh, that's just the way they are."

When you auditioned did he say to you, "I have enough white comics"? 'Cause that was his favorite line to people.

No. We said that to him before he said that to us. I went into his office and I said to him, "Lemme guess, you have enough white comics already?" So I diffused the situation by saying that, and he just burst out laughing, and I knew I was in.

So Lucien actually passed you then?

I think Richie actually passed us first and told us we could play the club during the week, and then Lucien was the one who passed us for the weekends and shit. After that first night that Richie saw us, we were able to call in our avails, and most of the spots were late night. And we were here every fuckin' night for late night. Late night was Sundays through Thursdays after eleven, and we were usually like the first people to sign in. And once you signed in, you had to stay. If you left, you lost your spot. That was Lucien's rule, and he was very strict about that.

Do you remember your first Saturday night performing at The Strip?

Oh, yeah. My first weekend here, I got some shows on Friday and Saturday, so Friday got me ready for Saturday, because Saturday was really fuckin' amazing. That's where you see the room, every seat in the house was packed—I mean *packed*. And then you see the crowds going out the door, and me and Tony would sit in that booth out front and watch the crowds, and then we'd be like, "Okay, let's go in the back and get ready." And we'd go and prepare, and it was exciting, man. It was like performing at Carnegie Hall. It was crazy.

Who were some of the people you came up with?

Steve Byrne was around. Jessica Kirson, Godfrey, Ardie Fuqua, who came up once in a while. Steve Donovan, who was a good friend of mine; and Rachel Feinstein, who used to be my roommate. Me and Rachel got an apartment on 75th Street off of 1st Avenue, because it was this close to

The Strip. Buddy Bolton was also living there and saw an apartment open, and Jeannie and Mariel . . . Jeanie's husband was the building manager, and they got me the apartment. So I got my first apartment in Manhattan through The Comic Strip. I didn't even realize that till I just said it.

And how did you make the transition to TV because you've been on so many shows.

The first time I got anything for television was here, at a bringer show for Jeannie and Mariel. There was an agent in the room from Paradigm, and he saw me, and he came over to me afterward and told me he wanted to start sending me on stuff freelance. I can't think of his name, but he was a big agent, and I can see his dumb face in my mind.

So they started sending me out, and within a week and a half I booked a national commercial—and that's how I got to be able to afford the apartment around the corner. It was for Southwest Airlines, and I was a band member in the wrong city, and it was pretty funny. It was a good face shot of me, so it got my mother off my back, it got me healthcare, it got me in SAG, and it got me an apartment, and that all came from The Comic Strip.

Do young guys today still want to perform at The Strip?

Absolutely. Not only young guys, but guys who have already made it love to come back and perform at The Strip. They know that all roads lead through The Strip. That's why I was so upset when I heard that late night wasn't around anymore. You gotta have late night 'cause that's that young fuckin' thing that it gives the club and makes people wanna hang out here. That's what made this club different from other clubs and made it viable to hang out, 'cause you knew you might get onstage. I used to double my spots just by hanging out.[20]

---

[20] Jeffrey Gurian's note: I can vouch for that since I now host late night on Sundays and Mondays, and Sherrod's cousin Jordan Rock hosts Wednesdays and Thursdays.

Last thing. Tell me about Richie Tienken.

Richie's always been great. We looked at him like an icon, a legend. When Chrissy used to have his *Cops 2* leather jacket, me and Tony used to fight over who would wear that shit to school, and we used to watch the movie all the time, and Richie appeared in the last scene of the movie as Mr. Anderson, and he would say his line: "Who's that black guy?" It was always funny to us to know that Chrissy knew these people and that they cared about Chrissy and that Richie had helped him start his career—and now I'm sitting here with the guy! It's just crazy. I'm so lucky. I just want this place to last forever, and I also want to state openly that if this place is ever up for sale, me and Tone get the first bid!

Tony Rock[21]

Tony Rock is a comedian and actor with a national and international presence. Tony has been a regular on TV and in films, and he starred in the Will Smith-created show on UPN called *All Of Us* from 2003 to 2007 and his own show *The Tony Rock Project.* He was featured in the movie *Hitch,* as well as *Three Can Play That Game, Life Support,* and *Think Like A Man.* He is the new host of Jamie Foxx's *Apollo Live* on Centric TV.

When did you start performing comedy, and what are your earliest memories of The Comic Strip?

Well, we started doing stand-up the same exact date, January 27, 1998. It was a bringer show, where you have to bring two people, so we got a third-party friend of ours to pay to watch me, and Sherrod paid to watch me. Then the third-party friend paid to watch Sherrod, and I paid to watch

---

21   In what I thought was a very funny and endearing manner, Tony *also* answered most of his questions in the "we" form, as did his cousin Sherrod Small. They were life-long friends who started performing on the exact same day and have experienced their careers so closely that they automatically answer questions about their lives and careers in "we." It was hysterical!

Sherrod, and that's how we got around it. We counted as each other's "bringer," and we've been in the game ever since.

We calculated that we would go one club at a time, so we wouldn't go after the next comedy club until we were both accepted in the first comedy club. And The Comic Strip was the first club.

How old were you at that time, and what had you been doing up until then?

I was twenty-six, and before that I was just working regular jobs. But I was "the funny guy" at every single job I had. I was the guy where people would go, "This guy's so funny, what are you a comic or something? This guy should do stand-up."

They didn't know that that was something I dreamed about, that was a secret desire of mine, so just by saying that they were kind of giving me a push towards the business without knowing it.

Was your interest in comedy because of Chrissy [Tony's brother, Chris Rock]?

No, not at all. You know what was weird . . . even as a kid, I always had an interest in comedy. But then when Chrissy got into the game, he kind of bred me to be a comic. Chrissy is six years older than me. He *made* me listen to Richard Pryor albums and made me listen to Dick Gregory, and every Saturday he would be, "We have to sit in front of this TV and watch Eddie Murphy on *SNL.*" I'm like the Frankenstein monster to Chrissy's Dr. Frankenstein. He *made* me be a comic. I really had no choice whatsoever.

So you're the funny guy at all of your jobs, but what were you doing to prepare for your first time onstage?

I actually used to write jokes down at work all the time. I don't even know why, maybe because Chrissy always taught me to have that comic mind. So when I saw something funny, I would just write it down, having no intention of sharing it with the world. Secretly, I think I did, but not really on a conscious level.

But when I told Chrissy I was really gonna pursue it 100 percent, he told me just to get ready for all the stuff I was gonna hear coming behind him, all the negative stuff like, "He's not really funny, he's just trying to follow his brother," or, "He just passed at The Comic Strip because he's Chris's brother," or, "He's just using his name to sell tickets." So I prepared myself for a whole year before I actually got onstage.

Was it Chris who told you about The Strip?

No, I knew about The Strip my whole life. I used to come in as a teenager and sit in the back and watch Chrissy onstage. I knew Lucien, I knew Richie, some of the staff, and Jim Mendrinos, who used to host the bringer shows.

Open mic night in those days was Saturday at six p.m. Audition night was Monday night at about eight p.m. And as far as what kind of stuff I was performing in those days, it was kind of always the same. My comedy has always been sort of fun, just a good time, intertwined with like racial obser-vations, so like one of my earlier jokes was like, "There was a new network called BET, Black Entertainment Television, but it's so low budget that it's just remakes of old white television shows with an entirely black cast.

So it's like Fantasy Island with all black people. Gary Coleman is Tattoo, and Billy Dee Williams is Mr. Roarke. You couldn't do Brady Bunch because it would be unbelievable to think that three black boys would be sleeping in the very next room to three black girls that were no relation to them and they weren't trying to have sex."

And that was my big bit. I felt like a king when I did that bit. That was the "bring 'em home" joke.

So what was your first time onstage at The Strip like?

There were maybe fifteen people in the audience. In those days, you had to be passed by Starla before you could even get to see Lucien. Maybe five or ten other comics were there. Sherrod, Steve Donovan, Rachel Feinstein, who I'm still friendly with to this day. A guy named Terry McNally was the host. And there were a few guys who came from my job who wanted to see what it would be like. It was very exciting.

I thought I was good, and we both thought we should have been allowed to do the ten o'clock show immediately. Every comic knows that the ten o'clock show on Friday or Saturday is the pinnacle of stand-up in New York City. If you do the ten o'clock show, that's your call up to "the bigs." So we knew we were ten o'clock comics. Now, everybody else has to see it.

After we were done with our sets, Sherrod and I hugged on the corner and we cried. We literally cried. The corner of 81st Street and 2nd Avenue. I called my mother to tell her. It was everything me and Sherrod had thought about the entire summer that led up to that point. The culmination of all the hard work had paid off that night.

Do you remember the night you asked Richie to watch you perform and he said, "I'm only gonna tell you one of two things. Either you can keep your last name or you have to change it."

Yeah, I remember, and I was offended too. I was offended because I thought to myself, "Wait a minute, this is my father's name, Rock, not just Chrissy's name." Even though Chrissy established the name in comedy, it's still my family name. So I kind of was offended, but I understood where he was coming from. So he went up and watched me, and I come offstage, and he always calls me "Kid," and so he gave me the little Mafioso tap on the cheek, and he says, "Hey, kid, you can keep your name!"

And then he even asked to manage me. He came in one night, I think it was a Friday or Saturday show, and after I went up he called me in this little office and he said, "You know what, I'm startin' to get the bug again. I'm startin' to feel that excitement about comedy again because of you, and we should work together." And I felt great 'cause I love this guy. It was an amazing, amazing feeling. It was just validation for all the hard work I put in. Just passing The Strip, and Lucien saying that I deserved to be here, and Richie saying he wanted to manage me, it was complete and total validation.

Plus I was a *huge* Eddie Murphy fan, and here was the guy who managed Eddie Murphy wanting to manage me. I kind of felt like the heir to the throne when I would come in the club after that, 'cause Richie chose to manage this kid over everybody else. It really made me feel kind of special.

Who were some of your contemporaries when you started out at The Strip?

Sherrod Small, Rachel Feinstein, Steve Donovan, Rich Bradley, David J. Nash, and Mike Young, both of whom I did the Montreal Comedy Festival with in like 2000. Richie told me to audition for it in '99, and I said, "If I pass on it this year and wait till next year, I'll be that much stronger as a comic." And I'm glad I did that, and Richie agreed. So 2000, I auditioned for Montreal, got it, and of course went up with Sherrod, who came to support me. Then in 2001, I was chosen by *Variety Magazine* as one of the top ten young, up-and-coming comics in the country.

So waiting that year really paid off. We were calculating, and we knew what we were doing. We also passed on a holding deal from UPN that year. They wanted me to sign a holding deal, and I didn't see the point of it 'cause a holding deal takes you off the market. If they couldn't find a project that was right for me, I'd wind up sitting on the shelf for a year. So we decided to pass. And they offered me like $200,000 to start. I said, "No," and they came back the next morning and said $250,000, which was like a big thing. But I said "no" again, and they said, "Well, the deal's off the table at midnight." And I was like, "Well, if the deal's off the table at midnight, it's off the table at midnight. So be it, 'cause I still could go home and do stand-up." But the cool thing about Richie is that he always made decisions with me together. He'd say, "Let's think about this, kid."

Then, after we passed on the holding deal, we came back home and the Oxygen deal happened. I hosted a TV show on Oxygen called *Can You Tell?* It was kind of a hipper version of *What's My Line?*

So how long were you performing before you finally got to audition for Lucien?

It was maybe November or December of the year I started performing. I auditioned for Starla first, and she said right away, "Come back next week and you'll audition for Lucien. I want him to take a look at you."

That was kind of quick, don't you think?

We *lived* in here. We stayed in here every single day. We knew that would expedite the process because we knew we were always gonna be in your face. Wherever you looked, you'd see us. If somebody didn't show up and you needed a comic, it was like, "These guys didn't pass yet, but damn, we need a comic to go up." So we stayed, and we thought to ourselves, "Either we're gonna make people sick of us, or they're gonna love us."

I had one joke about being in prison. Something like, "I have a cousin who's in prison. He's on Death Row. He's like, 'I'm not fearing death, because when I die, Jesus is gonna be standing there holding my hand. And when they put me in that electric chair, Jesus is gonna be there holding my hand.' And I'm like, 'Oh yeah, well, when they throw that switch, Jesus is gonna let go and jump out of the way, and go, "I already died for your sins, now it's *your* turn!"'" And Lucien said to me when I got off, "If you could write jokes like that, that means you could write *more* jokes like that and you're in. You can call in your avails, and welcome to The Comic Strip." And that's my Lucien story of how I passed my audition at The Strip.

Tell me about Richie Tienken.[22]

Richie took a chance on me. He didn't have to do that. He had the club, he had a successful run with Eddie for eleven years, and he didn't

---

22 At this memory, Tony's eyes filled with tears.

have to take a chance on me. But yet he did. He gave me a shot, and he changed my life. Nobody knew who I was, and he gave me that chance and took a shot. I was just this dude's brother, you know what I mean? It doesn't validate who I am as a comic. And Richie took a chance on me, and my life's never been the same ever since.

And so how would you like to sum up your whole Comic Strip experience?

I started here, I bombed here, I got standing ovations here, I learned how to be a comic here. I'll be forever loyal to The Strip . . . and I thank Lucien. Lucien told me when I got offstage in Montreal, he came up to me and said, "There's nothin' more I can do for you. That was your introduction to the world. The world will know who Tony Rock is from now on." And that was it. So the world knows who Tony Rock is thanks to The Comic Strip.

Pete Dominick

Pete Dominick is a comedian and radio talk show personality. Aside from head-lining nationally, he's the warm-up comic for *The Colbert Report* and has been the warm-up act for *The Daily Show* more than one hundred times. Pete's successful appearance at the Just For Laughs festival in Montreal led Sirius Radio to offer him his own show, *Comedy By Request*, and he was soon hosting a second show called *Getting Late with Pete Dominick*. He currently does a daily three-hour show called *Stand Up with Pete Dominick*.

When did you start performing, and what were your earliest memories of The Comic Strip.

I started in '96; I think it was July. I was still in school. I always consider my career really got started somewhere in the late '90s, when I got done with school. But definitely I did go up onstage in New York in '96. I was in acting school. I did two years in college, and then I came to New York to do two years at The American Musical and Dramatic Academy, which was a tremendous waste of money. Studying acting always seems like a waste of money. Any time someone tells me they're spending money on acting classes, I always say, "Leonardo DiCaprio," who I'm pretty sure never took any acting classes. And he's done well!

I came to The Comic Strip as an audience member with a buddy of mine and stayed here from start to finish. I saw Johnny Lampert, Louis CK, and this guy who *still* does late night. I won't say his name, but he did late night then, and he still does it now!

Lucien had the idea that once you passed the club, you could always do late night, and the great thing about that policy was that it weeded out those who didn't want it bad enough. You'd come here on a Sunday or Monday, and you'd wait all night 'cause he'd make you wait. You couldn't leave. You couldn't sign up at nine and come back at eleven. You'd have to stay or else you'd lose your spot. It was a brutal but effective policy because this business, stand-up comedy specifically, is not for those who aren't determined—and it's not for those who have any other choices as far as a career goes.

I always say, "If there's anything else you've got that you enjoy, and that you're good at, you should probably do that, because it's an awful business and a shitty lifestyle." A lot of people in the business don't find that out till later on. I always think I'm the happiest guy in the business. But it all depends on how you measure success. I know guys who are much more "successful" than me, who have been doing stand-up for the same amount of time I have, but they're miserable. You look at a guy like David Letterman. He doesn't seem happy. Dave Attell, who's one of the greatest comedians of all time . . . his HBO special was called *Captain Miserable.*

So how do you transition from being an audience member to a performer?

I had performed in college at a talent show before that night in the audience at The Strip. And even in high school, I hosted the talent shows doing impressions of George Bush, Ross Perot, and even Clinton. It's a funny thing, I was the best in impressions in Syracuse, New York, and then I moved to New York City and was the *worst* at impressions. I moved from the pond to the ocean. New York has the most talent in the comedy business, so I soon came to realize that my Forrest Gump was fairly unoriginal.

I think I always knew I wanted to be a stand-up from the time I was very young, which has been an advantage for me. You see some people who first start when they're like twenty-seven. So the first club I did in the city was Stand-Up New York. And I made that my home club, because I lived on the Upper West Side near the club, I worked in a gym, and I had to do the bringer shows, and all the members of the gym lived in the area, so it made it easy for me to get new members of the gym to come in to see me perform.

Of course, after they saw me they would never come again, but I could always get fresh faces at that gym. I worked at the front desk, and I was also a personal trainer, so I got to meet a lot of people. I worked there for about seven years and made a pretty good living while having a pretty good time. The one thing my father taught me was to find a job you enjoy doing.

Personal training actually held me back from having success in stand-up comedy because I enjoyed it so much. You tend to have more success in stand-up if you're really miserable in your day job. But it wasn't that way for me. It was a really good job, all my clients were rich and well-known influential people, and I got laid a lot. I never got laid before that, and I started working in a gym and all of a sudden I'm fucking forty-year-old women. So that was nice 'cause I like the cougars!

But The Comic Strip and The Comedy Cellar are the two clubs in New York City that have the greatest reputations in the business. Even the guys in LA, most of them started here. So The Strip is really the most famous club in existence. It's history and it's policies, especially under Lucien . . . he didn't pass Jon Stewart, and I don't think he passed Dennis Miller, and there's other well-known people who still hold a grudge against Lucien, and trying to get that guy to like you was just the hardest thing in the world. Especially if you were a white guy. Every white guy heard the line, "I've got enough white guys right now. I need something different from you." So when he passed me, that's a story in itself.

The first time Lucien ever saw me perform I was auditioning for the Montreal comedy festival. It was on a Saturday night, and I just destroyed the audience. I get offstage, and I hear Lucien from the booth, "Very good job." So that put me on the map. That was not technically an audition for the club, because it was an audition for Montreal, but at least he got to see me. And the funny thing was, it was more important to pass for Lucien than it was to pass for the festival where the entire industry shows up.

I wound up performing for six or seven years before Lucien passed me. Starla was this woman who, for some reason, was judging comedians, which was always strange to all of us, because she wasn't a great comedian, and I don't mind saying that on the record. Not only wasn't she a great comedian, but she wasn't even a really good comedian. You take a guy like Moody McCarthy who would fill in for her . . . great comedian, technically sound, and really good guy who knew how to let you down.

The first time I ever auditioned here I did it through the legitimate way, which was the lottery system that they used, and Starla had positive things to say to me afterwards. If she didn't pass you first, Lucien wouldn't watch you. That was his way of weeding out the people who weren't that good.

I was a hack for a long time. Luckily I had a lot of good mentors or else I wouldn't have even known. When you first start out, you're thinkin' if you're getting laughs you should be getting work. But anybody can get laughs. You can go up and do somebody else's act and get laughs if you're a good actor. But you have to have original material and persona and timing and technique and style and energy . . . there's a million things that go into it.

I came back, after having performed for a few years, and I sat down with Lucien, and I basically convinced him to pass me, to give me the number. I said, "Listen you gotta pass me." And he said, "Okay, here's the number to leave your avails." And once he gives you the number to leave your avails, you can consider yourself passed. I'll always remember that moment. And it was that monkey off my back, and it was such a big deal. That's when being accepted at The Comic Strip put you on the map of all the other comedy clubs in New York, because The Comic Strip always posted their schedule somewhere, so all the bookers would see the names. They had it online and also on the phone number so you could call and find out who was performing. But you didn't even need that. Once you're working at a comedy club in New York, everybody who needs to know knows you're there.

But make no mistake, no matter what any comedian tells you, passing at The Comic Strip, certainly when Lucien was alive, was the ultimate. And I think I was one of the last ten guys that Lucien passed, before *he* passed. After he passed me, I thought I might be the last guy, because he was so sick at the time, but then he lasted a little over another year. When he died, part of New York comedy died with him. He was definitely a legend.

And I'm not gonna lie to you, he was never one of my favorite guys, but I respected his authority and his taste, because in this business you have to be nice to people you don't like. Case in point: I can't stand you Jeffrey, but I really want to be in this book![23]

Tell me about Richie Tienken.

I had seen Richie, but he was almost never here during the week. He would come in on the weekends, but I didn't get spots on the weekends. So I didn't see him much.

You didn't get spots because you weren't available or because you were new and they weren't offered to you?

No one is not available for a weekend spot at The Comic Strip. There are times now when I'm here on a Saturday night to do two shows, and in between shows, before I go up onstage, I often remind myself, "Remember, you wanted this. Don't take this for granted." One dream was to be passed at The Comic Strip, and the other dream was to work here on a Saturday. A Friday is nice, but there's nothing better than Saturday night at The Strip. And I opened for Artie Lange in front of 6,000 people, and it's not nearly as much fun as The Comic Strip on a Saturday night.

But let me tell you how I met Richie because that was very cool. He saw me perform. That's the way I wanted to meet Richie. I didn't want to meet him because he heard about me. I didn't want to meet him by introduction. I wanted him to see me perform. And it just so happened that he saw me doing a set, in which something happened in the audience where he got to see my strongest skill, which is an improvisational moment with the audience. After the set, he walked up to me and introduced himself and told me he thought it was hysterical what I did. It was one of those times when you have a brilliant moment and usually no one important is there to see it. This time someone was there.

---

[23] Thank God he was laughing when he said that!

Jeffrey Ross

Jeffrey Ross, aka "The Roastmaster General," is not only a comedian but also an actor, director, and author. In addition to his Comedy Central special *No Offense*, he has appeared in the last nine Comedy Central Roasts, which led to his book, *I Only Roast the Ones I Love*. Jeffrey's film, *Patriot Act: A Jeffrey Ross Home Movie*, about his trip to Iraq to entertain the troops with Drew Carey and Kathy Kinney, won Best Feature Film at the Montreal Comedy Festival. He was a contestant on *Dancing with the Stars* and has guest-starred on TV shows such as *Six Feet Under*, *The Sarah Silverman Program*, and *Weeds*.

So when did you first start performing, and what are your earliest memories of The Comic Strip.

I started performing the year that you bought those sunglasses. I guess it was around 1989 that I did my first open-mic night, about the same time those Capezios [white shoes Jeffrey Gurian was wearing] were in fashion.[24]

I started doing open mics in Times Square at a place called The Ye Old Tripple Inn. I made my first twenty bucks there, and I would start to get regular spots there too. The key thing for me was I was driving in from Jersey, so it didn't pay for me to do one spot at Catch, so it became a mission for me to get into The Comic Strip. That way I could double up without even having to move my car.

---

[24] It was around that time I realized I was being roasted by Jeffrey Ross. Not the worst thing in the world for a comic.

I had always heard that if you worked The Comic Strip you could work everywhere. That was the club to pass, and that was my goal. If you could "kill" at The Comic Strip then you could pretty much headline at any comedy club. It had a certain prominence, and you wanted to conquer that.

It took a long time, but I finally got an audition where I got Lucien to watch me. And he cut me off. He had me sit down in the club, and it was all very new to me. At the time I was auditioning wherever I could to try and get a name for myself, so auditioning for Lucien was a big deal.

He himself only saw people once in a blue moon. He certainly didn't need comics. To get an audition you really had to get your shit together. And this would definitely not be the first club you got into. You had to have some experience first before you could crack The Strip. You needed some swagger. You had to be killing. There's no other room that you could just crush in like this room. The laughs just reverberate here. If Lucien even spent time watching and analyzing your act, it was a big deal and meant you were moving up a notch as a city comic.

Lucien was encouraging to me. He gave me a pep talk and said in very matter-of-fact terms whether he could use you or not. So by doing that, he gave you something to work toward, knowing that at least he felt he could use you somewhere down the road, even if it wasn't right now. In this business you sort of have to set your own goals, and Lucien sort of set that out for me, so I owe him a debt of gratitude for that. Just the fact that he would take the time to pontificate about you and your act meant a lot, because he was the number one expert. He had seen them all come and go. By the time I got here, he had already had huge stars come out of this place, so he had a huge reputation with the comics. It was really big for me.

So I got passed at The Comic Strip and was asked to call in my avails, but I didn't get any spots for a while. But just getting passed was a very prestigious credit that allowed you to get booked for money on the road or at other clubs. Just the fact that Lucien would ask you to call in your avails was like a demarcation in your career.

And I don't remember exactly who started out with me here, but the funniest black comics were always at The Comic Strip. I don't know why but for whatever reason, it seemed to nurture that type of talent, from Brooklyn and uptown, and it was really fun to see people breaking out.

It was a really cool place to hang out by the bar. I remember Chris Rock getting booked on *SNL*, and one night, shortly afterwards he pulled up in his bright, cherry red Corvette. And I was so impressed, I'm like, "Oh man, that's so cool. That guy made it. He came out of The Comic Strip, and there he is a superstar just stopping by to say 'hi' to the inmates."

I remember watching Sarah Silverman coming in here and always trying out crazy stuff, and Jim Breuer doing a bit about drinking tequila, and every night people would just go berserk for that bit. I think his ten-minute bit on drinking probably sold more drinks than anything else in the place.

It's funny what you remember. They would have regular showcases here, so Lucien would make out a list of sometimes as many as twenty comics doing five minutes each, and executives from television shows and movies and commercials and casting people would come and watch. Whoever the newer faces were, they would always get put up on these shows. That was always fun.

I had a white Jeep, and I would travel in every night from Springfield, New Jersey. I tried to double up as much as I could, so I tried to get a spot at Catch and The Strip and get as much stage time and toll money as possible. That twenty bucks was a big deal then. Plus if you got an early spot at The Strip, like nine or so, you could still get downtown and get a spot for a free meal somewhere else, so it was important for me to get to The Strip early. The first hour of that show was always amazing.

Sometimes before a roast, I'll come down here to try out my jokes, and I'll take one of the audience members and bring them up onstage and have them sit here and play whoever I'm roasting. That way, I can get a feel for how strong the material is. Inevitably, they work better at The Strip than they do the night of the real roast, because this place is like a barn. The laughter just reverberates off the walls. You can wind up doing half as many jokes, but the laughs take so long that the set stretches out where you wind up with twenty minutes. I think the shape has a lot to do with it. It's like a little box, and everybody's looking that way [toward the stage], so the laughs just hit the stage and then they bounce off that brick wall and come back into the audience, so they feel it from every angle. Low ceiling, they keep it nice and cool, and except for all these ugly decorations, it's perfect. This is a great room to write in and a great environment for trying out jokes, because the audience is already laughing at your setups. That way, you have time to feel out a new punch line.

When you're here on the weekends you don't wanna try out too much new stuff—you just wanna kill. But when you're here during the week, it's a different story. It's more relaxed. Sometimes I'll even take out my notes, and it's a great place to try out my roast jokes because the audience is so close to the stage, so for a comedian who makes fun of people, it's a perfect setup.

The Comic Strip is definitely an entertainment landmark, and it's just really cool to be part of it.

Jim Gaffigan

By his own description, Jim Gaffigan is a pale Korean actor, comedian, and writer whose laidback style has made him one of the five most successful stand-up comedians touring the country today. His CDs and DVDs have reached platinum sales, and his writing and voice-over work for Conan O'Brien's animated series, *Pale Force,* led to nominations for both a Broadband Emmy and a Webby Award. Jim is also a star of TV and film, including *Welcome to New York, Flight of the Conchords, Law & Order, Going the Distance, Away We Go,* and *Salvation Boulevard.*

What year did you start performing, and what are some of your earliest memories of The Comic Strip?

I started performing and doing stand-up right about 1990, maybe around June was when I first did a show in a club. My very first show was doing improv in the National Improvisational Theatre, and I had always kind of wanted to do stand-up. Stand-up at that time was all over TV, you know, like *Evening At The Improv* and things like that.

I essentially waited for one of my improv friends in my class to kind of challenge me to do stand-up. It's a little bit of a blur. Not because of any substance abuse, just because it was a long time ago. This friend of mine challenged me to do stand-up. He had read Judy Carter's book, and we met once or twice a week and cobbled together a set and finally went up onstage at Rose's Turn, which at the time was called something else, which I can't remember now, but it was where Woody Allen did his first stand-up.

So this guy challenged me to do this comedy seminar class, and then on the final performance he never showed up. But I did. So that night at Rose's Turn, it went very well. I had memorized every reaction, every inclination, and it was an incredibly safe room. Basically I performed in a show with people who essentially, like myself, were doing stand-up for the first time. It was not that much of a challenge. It was lined up to succeed. It was a supportive room and an incredible experience. And I remember how rewarding it felt to know that my material was decent and that I had a shot at this. Originally, I just wanted to do stand-up and thought maybe I would write on the *David Letterman Show*. It never occurred to me that it could lead to anything special.

To backstep a minute, I was the only one in New York. The rest of my family was in Indiana, and being from Indiana, if you were gonna go to a big city it would probably be Chicago. There was really kind of no reason to go to New York or LA.

But I had fallen in love with New York back while I was growing up watching *The Odd Couple*. I was a really pale kid, in a really white community, so I was kind of the oddball ironically. So I wanted to go where everyone's an oddball, and I feel that New York's that way.

When you started in 1990 had you heard of The Comic Strip? Was it a goal of yours to perform here?

The Comic Strip was definitely one of the good clubs. I came into this relatively ignorant. I did stand-up first, and then I learned about what clubs were around. I knew there was Catch A Rising Star, The Improv, The Comic Strip and The Cellar, and Stand-Up New York, but I don't remember when I learned about any of them. So when I started there still was the conventional wisdom of passing at The Improv, which was a big rite of passage, like passing at The Comic Strip was a big rite of passage. Those were the two places where you would pass, and it was a stepping stone to becoming a comedian.

Then there was the lottery in order to get onstage. I auditioned for Lucien, who was this incredibly intimidating figure. The great cruelty about stand-up is that it is a meritocracy—but it's also within the entertainment industry, which is all bullshit and lies, you know? And perception. Let me explain it this way: The entertainment business is something that nobody can figure out. And stand-up comedy is even more confusing, because there's a bit of a meritocracy built in . . . whoever gets the laughs. Lucien was trying to pick the winner, and he was also trying to pick different types of winners. Like one guy might be good on *Letterman*, another comic might be the type that could break out in an HBO special, another one might have an incredible likeability, and so he had to kind of identify that.

I remember getting onstage, and I remember thinking I had passed because in stand-up you have to have what I call an un-deniability. I've been very blessed and very lucky, and I've also had an enormous amount of feeling "it's not fair that I didn't get things," in my view. But there's a lot of things where, eventually, I just had to get to the point where I just did stand-up because I love it, not for what I can get from it. I wish I could say, "I enjoy making people happy," but I really enjoy coming up with a new joke for myself.

And so, I had an expectation that I would eventually get passed at The Comic Strip but I felt like . . . the process of getting passed back then was going in on Monday night, and you'd do four or five minutes, and the MC would determine whether you were ready to see Lucien. The couple of times I did it, I was not deemed ready to see Lucien. I also realized that you had to go about getting recommendations from other comics who had already passed, so there was a bit of a sense of drama and corruption, even in just getting seen by Lucien.

Anyway, I had a good set, but I still didn't get bumped up to where Lucien would see me. Which was fairly traumatic. Eventually I got seen by Lucien and I think he said I wasn't ready, and then eventually I got passed. I remember walking offstage and realizing that Lucien *had* to pass me. I'd come close before, and I had new material, and the audience validated me in a way that was undeniable. I had a comedy mentor when I was starting. Really my only credit the first six years I was doing stand-up was that Dave Attell thought I was funny. I think Dave was like a mentor to me. Calling him a "supporter" would be a little ironic for those of us who know him. But then again, we're all a little "broken" in stand-up.

So the great irony is that I kind of knew when I was getting offstage that night at The Strip that I had more or less passed. I knew it wasn't the answer. You know you have this romantic notion when you start stand-up, like, "I got five minutes. Let's do *Letterman* now!" And that gets beaten out of you pretty quick.

In my mind, there's generations and mini-generations of comedians in stand-up. There was the Dave Attell, Louis CK, Kevin Brennan, Todd Barry class. Then above that, there was a whole other class of comedians. And then in my class there was Greg Giraldo, Judah Friedlander, Bonnie McFarlane, Ian Bagg—we were all in this individual class. And yeah, there was people who overlapped, and essentially it's kind of a mess now.

After I passed at The Strip, it started the whole drama of whether you were gonna get a spot or whether you were gonna go on at a certain time, and it would just be a bloodbath when you were just starting out. Especially because, in retrospect, stylistically I don't know that I was right for the room. I've always been this slow-talking Midwesterner, as opposed to the fast-talking New Yorkers. And this was when Lucien was still papering the room, which was one of the ways he kept The Comic Strip alive, by just filling it.

What did it mean to you to pass The Strip?

It was very important to me to pass The Strip because it was a room where working comics worked. There was a legitimacy to working at The Comic Strip. It's like Lucien was a carpenter and there was a practicality almost to his peculiarities. There wasn't anyone going onstage that he just had a hunch on. He may have had a hunch, but he knew they could pull off a couple of minutes. I mean, it could be a bloodbath on the weekends, like if a comic had to follow someone really strong, that comic might die a miserable death.

The entertainment industry is really a pursuit of insanity. The best way I can explain it is to say that passing at The Strip was an incredible sense of relief. I feel like, in retrospect, the ironic thing, considering how lucky I've been in my career, is that aside from *Caroline's Comedy Hour*, I was the last one of my peer group to actually get anything. I was the last one to get into The Strip, I was the last one to appear on a late-night talk show, I was the last one to middle on the road. There was definitely a lot of pressure on me. Stylistically, I was slower and quieter and more mundane in my topic matter. I'm also a white guy and the last thing they needed, as Lucien would often say, was another white guy. That's not to say I haven't been very lucky.

I get these incredible gifts to me, but I feel like they're separated by incredible injustice, you know what I mean? I think what I'm trying to say is that I've paid my dues. I think no one would say I got where I got because I'm good looking or because they were looking for a pale, white guy, and I don't mean that in any racial sense, 'cause that could sound very weird. I would literally have to wait for Kevin Brennan, Todd Barry, Louis CK, and Dave Attell to be out of town for me to even possibly *get* a spot! And if there was a spot open, you know Giraldo is more polished, was more likeable, was certainly more confident, so I would *never* get the spot. So it was one of those things where I wouldn't change it, but I really early on had to stand-up just for the love of it, because there was no real sign that anything good was ever gonna happen for me.

So in closing, I think The Comic Strip was very informative in the development of my career, but in some ways it was a bus station filled with comics and this eccentric, Lucien Hold, so when I came in to get spots they were few and far between, and as I got to know my style of stand-up, it became apparent to me that the audience at The Strip was much younger, and if I followed someone really filthy it would be a struggle. If I went on early they would still be seating people. So The Comic Strip definitely had a big influence in my development, curing me of stage fright, and in my overall development, but it also taught me where I didn't belong.

I think The Strip was where I cut my teeth and where I went through a lot of frustration, which led to a certain kind of detachment to stand-up. There was an arc to my attitude to stand-up that definitely evolved here, starting from being driven, to scrapping to passing, to trying to get spots to eventually just the detachment of just doing stand-up for the sake of doing stand-up. I don't know if that makes any sense, but I hope it does.

Judah Friedlander

Judah Friedlander is an actor, comedian, and author who started in show business as the cameraman for a short on Chris Rock called *Who Is Chris Rock?* With his trademark look of trucker's hats, oversized glasses, and wild hair, he's been in films like *Meet The Parents*, *Zoolander*, and *American Splendor*. He's appeared on VH1's *Best Week Ever* and on the hit series *30 Rock*. His newly released book is *How To Beat Up Anybody: An Instructional and Inspirational Karate book by The World Champion*.

When did you first start working the clubs in New York?

When I was nineteen, I tried stand-up at Garvins, a club in D.C. I was already living in New York, but I went home to visit my parents in Maryland.

When I was around twenty, I started doing open mics here in the city. Pretty much depressing open mics, for the most part. Like I remember Eagle Tavern was one of the ones. It was like a bar on 8th or 9th, in the basement, and was just other comedians waiting to go on and like three drunk guys at the bar.

The first comedy show I ever remember seeing was at Comedy U Grand. I had always wanted to come to The Comic Strip, but it seemed so far away. I was living in The Village on Broadway and 10th Street, in the dorm. Adam Sandler was actually in the same dorm I was in. He was a few years ahead of me. I think I was too shy to actually meet him, but I remember once I talked to one of his partners, Tim Herlihy, who used to write bits with him and went on to work on a lot of his movies. Sandler was already pretty big. He hit it really young. He was a regular here at The Strip—he was already doing *Remote Control* and was a regular on *The Cosby Show*.

I first probably did *The Lottery* audition at The Comic Strip in 1989 or '90, not thinking that you should probably go onstage more than three times before auditioning at The Comic Strip. Back then, I had no idea. Coming to The Comic Strip to audition on a Monday night was really intimidating at first. I remember back then, I think the lotteries were like once a month, and you'd line up on the street and there'd be like fifty to a hundred people in a line around the corner. Now I think you do it twice a year!

So, did you ever finally "pass" here?

It took me a while to get in. I think I passed in '93 or '94. I had already been playing other clubs. In 1991, I finished film school, and that's when I finally realized you're supposed to go out every night and do comedy. 'Cause the whole time I'd just been doing it a handful of times but still got a few paid gigs at some bars and stuff around the city. I was doing really well most of the time. In the beginning, you might have two sets where you completely destroy and then a third set where it doesn't go that well 'cause you're just not as strong.

I can't remember how many times I went into the little office after my audition with Lucien and had "the talk." And that was very intimidating 'cause he would speak very slowly, or sometimes he wouldn't speak at all, so you'd just be forced to start talking. It always felt awkward and was a really good power play move that he had there.

I remember once being in the office with him. I had had a really good audition. And I remember him saying, "I thought you were really good. You're really funny, but we already have a lot of white guys." And then there'd be a guy on the screen, and he'd say, "You're definitely funnier than this guy and he's a regular here. But I just don't have any room right now." So instead of gettin' all pissed off, 'cause a lot of people get pissed off, and go, "That's not fair," and shit. I just look at it like, "All right, I gotta get even better."

So finally I said to myself, "Instead of keep going back to Lucien, I'm just gonna wait till the time's right." And then I think it got to the point where a few comics were like, "Dude, you gotta start working The Comic Strip." And I don't think he'd seen me in like a year or something like that.

During that time, I had had a whole bunch of different kind of day jobs. At some points, I was making enough money that I could just do comedy, but in order to do that I hadda go out of town, 'cause the comedy clubs out of town pay more than in town. But I also realized that if you're out of town all the time, you're kind of out of the TV and film game. Plus there's more better comics in town than out of town, and you kind of get better by your surroundings. If you go on shows with better comics, it kind of makes you a better comic.

I remember I had this one job just checking people into the gym. I hadda work from seven to four. So I'd work till four, go home, nap for two hours, then I'd go out and do as many shows as I could. There was

New York Comedy Club, Boston Comedy Club, The Strip, and I was pretty much working all the clubs including late night at The Comedy Cellar. I'd get home real late, sleep like three hours, and go back to the gym. So back in '92 or '94 when I finally passed at The Strip—I think John Busch recommended me and some other guys—so I went up, had a really good set, went into Lucien's office, and he just goes, "Well, here's the number. Call in your avails."

If you didn't pass The Strip, you'd still get shit from other comics: "This guy's not a real comic." That was definitely the vibe back then. This was the club that definitely kind of legitimized you. That was the way it felt. Plus my comedy history is really good, and I knew that Seinfeld and so many big stars came from here. This was also the club that would have the industry showcases, more so than the other clubs.

You have such a good hook. When did you come up with World Champion?

That's a good question 'cause it wasn't like a conscious thought. Whenever people do that, it's usually not genuine and it doesn't have legs. And you know on *30 Rock* I don't have a beard, but I think having the beard helps the World Champion character, because it's all about being the most macho, testosterone-filled beast. So he has to have a beard.

My act has always been very joke heavy. I've also always been very audience interactive, you know, playing the crowd. But I looked young for my age, so I was coming off as this young weirdo guy. Kind of like in the category of Steven Wright. Back then, most of the comics would sort of try and bond with the crowd. They'd be like, "Hey, I'm your best friend." Ever notice this? I decided to take the opposite approach and act like I'm just better than everyone.

Now Gladys [Simon]—who used to run a show at a place called Hamburger Harry's in Times Square but now runs the open mics at The Strip—I used to do her show, and one thing about New York is no matter how tough you are, when you come to New York, you get wimpy.

You could be the toughest guy in Europe, you come to New York, you turn into a wimp. So I decided just to make fun of 'em. I decided to use that room a lot, not to do my jokes, but just go up there, make fun of the crowd, act like I'm better than everyone, and just make up stuff on the spot.

And when I was a kid, I was always obsessed with breaking world records and was also very into art, so I started making my own hats. And this is probably mid- to late '90s. So I made one hat that said "Recordbreaker," because I was doing some jokes about me breaking all these ridiculous records.

So that's where the persona started to form, from my love of breaking records and the *Guinness Book of Records* when I was a kid, and then playing the crowd. And then at some point, after only having jokes about breaking records, and some athletic records, I decided to make a hat that said "World Champion," but not of what! Just like this idiot guy up there who was better than everyone at everything! That's why it was so cool that I got to accept the award from the *Guinness Book of Records* when The Strip had the longest running comedy show on record: fifty hours of comedy non-stop!

Do you remember first meeting Richie?

I always saw him around during the audition process, but Lucien was the guy you were always afraid of. Richie was intimidating only because he was the owner and carried that kind of respect, 'cause he was "the nice guy." But Lucien was the guy who was installing fear in everyone. He was the one you were always a little concerned about.

I first got to know Richie much better in more recent years, after Lucien passed, and he's always been really nice to me.

CHAPTER **THREE**

FRIENDS OF THE FAMILY

A successful comedy club cannot run on comedians alone. It takes other people to make it happen. In the case of The Comic Strip, there were three individuals we thought were important enough to not only mention, but also to give extra props to, because they were really instrumental in helping Richie's dream come to fruition.

Rory Rosegarten

What year did you get involved with comedy, and what are your earliest memories of The Comic Strip?

Nineteen eighty-three was the year I really started hammering away at a career, and I was also hanging out at The Comic Strip a lot. I had gone to school as a journalism major at Arizona State. They made me editor of the school newspaper as a freshman, and I was doing celebrity interviews, which I had also been doing for my high school newspaper and for various magazines. While I was there, *Playboy* asked me to do an interview with Robert Klein, and they actually flew me home during the school year to do that. So I met Klein, and I wound up leaving school after my second year because *Playboy* had offered me a full-time job.

Klein and I had remained close. He left Jack Rollins and Charlie Joffe [major managers who handled Woody Allen, Robin Williams, Billy Crystal, and stars of that magnitude], and I started working with him while I was working at *Playboy*. I signed Joe Bolster next, 'cause I had also interviewed him for a *Playboy* project, and then I signed Alan Colmes, and it was based on those three guys that I eventually left *Playboy* and opened my own company, which eventually became The Conversation Company. And I'm proud to say I still handle those three guys today, all these years later.

It didn't seem that hard to me to be a manager, but chalk that up to youthful naiveté. I was basically a young schmuck who thought I could do anything and that basically works in your favor sometimes. It certainly did in mine, 'cause if I really knew what it took, I probably wouldn't have tried, believing that I couldn't do it. But sometimes you luck into these things, and you either run or you don't, and in my case, I stayed around and took the reins, and here I am.

So, you get Robert Klein as a client. How did you get Joe Bolster and the rest?

I met Joe in kind of the same way I met Robert. It was kind of a promotion piece for *Playboy* on comedians and electronics . . . how about that for a combination? So anyway, I wheedled this comedians and electronics piece, and I called The Comic Strip. I didn't know Lucien at the time. I was young, and I didn't know a lot about comedians or the New York scene, and I wasn't officially a manager yet, so I called Lucien and asked him to recommend comedians for this piece. And the guys who were working at The Comic Strip in those days were guys like Joe Bolster, Paul Reiser, George Wallace, Dennis Wolfberg, John Hayman, all those guys that worked here were real comedians who had been working on a stage for years before anything happened for them.

So I called up Lucien Hold, and he was very friendly, and he introduced me to all these comics. In those early years Joe [Bolster] was known as the comedian's comedian. He was clean and sharp and fast, and other comedians would come into the room to watch his sets, and he would just crush—boom, boom, boom! There wasn't an extra "and," "the," or "but" in a sentence. It was just razor sharp and tight, and he was just great.

The testament to me was when Eddie Murphy hit it big, and Bob and Richie became Mr. Night and Mr. Day, as per *Rolling Stone Magazine.* Bob would take care of things during the day, and Richie would be out with Eddie and his friends at night. Even then, Richie, who was always with Eddie at nighttime, and they were inseparable, partly because it was fun and partly because they were the kings of New York and partly because Richie kept everybody out of trouble and on the straight and narrow. Richie would come in with that whole group. All the cars would double park on Second Avenue. No cops bothered anybody ever in that group, and Eddie would come in with his entourage. His bodyguards would come in first, then Richie and Uncle Ray would come in and look around, and then Eddie would make his entrance in some funky black leather outfit, dressed like a rock star, and Richie always, even in the midst of all this craziness, took the time to say hello to everyone.

And when I would come in here, I sat exactly where we're sitting now, in this little balcony alcove where the industry usually sits. This chair by the corner was the best view for me, and as a manager, what was starting to happen was that all the comedians wanted to talk to me and wanted to give me a tape. So it started to become a little overwhelming to me—flattering, of course—but a little overwhelming. So it was easier for me to sit right up here, because no one could get to me as easily.

Tell me about Lucien.

Well, in the early days Lucien was incredibly kind to me. I was a new manager working with Robert Klein, and Lucien was just always nice and very supportive. One of my most memorable nights here turned into day. I was sitting at the bar with Lucien, and of course in those days as a young manager, I was really looking up to him. Richie and Bob may have owned it, but Lucien was the face of the club, and he ran it well. So this night, I started talking to Lucien at the bar, and it must have been ten p.m. Before I knew it, ten became eleven, eleven became twelve, then two, then finally four in the morning, and I got in my car when the sun came up. I hadn't said one word the whole night. It was like an eight-hour soliloquy by Lucien Hold.

How did you meet Ray Romano? How did that come about?

I had been working with Brian Regan at the time, and Ray was right behind him. Everything that happened for Brian seemed to happen for Ray about a year later. I had seen Ray work, and I always thought he was great. Just great. And anyone who saw him then would say exactly the same thing. He worked here at The Strip; he worked The Cellar, Catch, The Improv. He worked all over town. In those days, everyone worked wherever they could. You may have had a home club, but you worked as many clubs as you could 'cause they only paid twenty bucks a set in those days. So when I wanted to manage Ray, Ray actually checked with Brian Regan 'cause they were friends from on the road. Brian gave me a thumbs up, and Ray and I started working together way, way back then. That was roughly 1987 or 1988.

Anything you want to add about The Comic Strip, Richie, Lucien, or anything else?

The Comic Strip didn't affect my life; it changed my life. The Comic Strip, for me, was the place I came to hang out with comedy guys. Then afterward we'd go to Gracie Mews, the diner up the block. And I remember just relishing just how cool it was. Here I was this schmucky guy in The Comic Strip, and the show would be over, and Wolfberg and Bolster were there, and we'd all just go. I would be there, and everybody would be riffing and shticking and laughing, and it was a fun time. It was before the business became a business.

David Eberhart[24]

You are actually the hero of this book, 'cause without you, The Comic Strip would have never been built. What made you do that?

It was a matter of enlightened self-interest! We had a tenant; he was already signed up. We obviously thought that they had a decent idea and that they could make some money and pay us our rent. But they couldn't

---

[24] David Eberhart is the landlord for The Comic Strip, and without him, the place would never have been built. Right before construction was about to start, all of Richie's construction money was stolen by a contractor and he would not have been able to continue had not David Eberhart, who is also a builder, stepped up to the plate.

do that without having the job done, and there wasn't anything extraordinarily complicated about any construction project if you know what you're doing. You start out by digging ditches, and I figured a couple of Irishmen oughta be able to do that!

What I do remember is that when we had to decide about doing a lease with these fellas, they told us about this bar/restaurant that they owned opposite Yankee Stadium. So Peter Dinkel and I went up there to check it out. We sat at the bar and had a beer, and we asked them for a menu, and they said they didn't have a menu. So then I said, "Where's your kitchen?" And they said, "We don't have a kitchen." This was the bartender talking. So then we said, "How do you cook?" Turns out they had a hot plate on the bar. I think the extent of their menu was making a melted cheese sandwich or something like that. So it wasn't on the strength of their culinary skills that they got me to write them a lease. But I guess there must have been something that appealed to us.

We must have thought that the idea they had had some credibility, and they probably told us all lies, but we believed enough of 'em so we went ahead with it. And the construction was pretty simple and basic: If they were told what they had to do one day at a time, they could pull it off. Plus, as I recall, Richie had a lot of friends who were in construction who helped him out as well. As a matter of fact, one of them almost accidentally knocked down the whole building by taking out a supporting wall in the back. We had to rush right over and put in a bunch of steel beams to hold the thing up!

Do you remember anything about Richie that stood out from those early days?

Well, we probably would have never done the deal with them if there wasn't something about the man that we found desirable.

Some of the biggest comedy stars in the world came out of there, and they all said that Richie had a great personality.

Well, I never noticed that! There was no question about the fact that we got along well, and we always had a good relationship.

Have you ever been to any shows at The Comic Strip?

Only one. I go once every thirty-five years. I have a feeling I must have missed some of the highlights.

What made you go the one time you went?

I guess I was kind of curious to see what these guys had done with the joint. It was probably within the first or second year the place was open. And I don't know of any great success stories that came out of the club within that time. I think the main reason we did this, aside from it sounding like a good idea, was that I was always intrigued by a challenge.

So about how long did it take for the place to be finished?

We thought we were gonna be open November of '75, and we wound up opening June of '76. We started building sometime in '74, so it took quite a while, with having to wait till everything was okayed by the building department and all.

Were you aware of what was happening in the club over the years and how many big stars were coming out of that place?

At one point, somebody told me that Richie had left town with some black guy, but they didn't say it was Eddie Murphy. [Richie interjected, laughing: "I'm sure it was my partner who spread that rumor!"] But that's when we heard that the guys were making the big time. I don't think I ever knew that Seinfeld came out of the club, but I was probably one of the 2 percent of the population that didn't watch the show.

How does it make you feel now that you know that if you hadn't stepped up, this place would not have been built and, in doing so, you changed the face of American comedy?

As I told Richie before you came in, if I hadn't done that, he might have done something that would have really made him successful!

Rick Newman

From what I understand, you opened Catch A Rising Star in 1973. Is that correct?

It was really the last two weeks of 1972, December 18, 1972. But for all intents and purposes, you could say it was 1973.

What were you doing before that led you to open a comedy club?

I'm a Bronx boy who went to what was then called The School of Industrial Arts. It has since turned into the School of Art and Design. I was from around Tremont and Prospect avenues, and I was the only kid in the neighborhood who wound up going to school outside The Bronx, and that changed a lot of things for me.

The guy that actually got me into the bar business was a guy named Danny Firestein, the toughest Jew in The Bronx. He wasn't afraid to fight anybody. He didn't care if you were one of the Fordham Baldies or the

Golden Guineas, which were two of the big Bronx gangs at the time. If anyone bothered any of the Jewish kids, he'd go beat the shit out of them. He got pretty far in the Golden Gloves at the time.

Originally, I thought I'd go into the advertising business, but then because I had a deep voice a lot of people told me I could be a DJ. I couldn't find a DJ school, but I went to an acting school and lost my Bronx accent. It was in acting school that I fell in love with the arts.

This guy Danny was a friend of my older brothers. He came home one night, found his wife with another guy, and went berserk, and felt that he had to leave New York for Vegas. He asked me to take over his bar, and I was just a kid, maybe like twenty years old. But he had a manager who gave me a crash course, and I did it. It was called Danny's Inferno, and I wound up putting in entertainment on certain nights, and business took off. Finally, Danny came back to town and said, "I don't know what you did but let's be partners and open a place in New York." So I wound up opening a place on 31st Street and 3rd Avenue. It was called The Clan 1890s. I was twenty-two years old, I owned my first bar, and it was a big success.

Due to my advertising background, I knew to always have a theme, which I used later on for Catch A Rising Star. Eventually, I wanted to be on my own. I found this location at 1487 First Avenue, between 77th and 78th streets. I wound up buying a place called Charlie Bates, and my original idea was to call it The Trading Post. I had come up with a bunch of potential names like Off-Off Broadway and The Talent Scout, but one night I was driving home and going over the 59th Street bridge and I heard the Perry Como song "Catch A Falling Star" and decided to change it to "Catch A Rising Star." And that was it.

A lot of my friends told me it was too long a name, so then I made it Rick Newman's Catch A Rising Star! I did that for the reason that in case Catch A Rising Star didn't last, at least people would remember Rick Newman for the next place that I opened.

So once you opened Catch, how did it turn into a comedy club?

I knew I wanted to do stand-up and music. My policy of putting acts on in those days was putting on two or three music acts and then a comedian, then two or three music acts and another comedian. Believe it or not, there weren't many good comedians in those days. It was nothing like it is today.

I know that Budd [Budd Friedman, founder of The Improv], thinks I took his idea for The Improv, but the truth is I never even thought about that. The way I structured Catch A Rising Star was all from what was in my mind, and it grew by the room telling me what to do. I like Budd a lot, I really do, but I kept that set-up for a long time.

Richard Belzer also came in kind of early on to audition, and I just saw that he was like amazing. He was able to just ad-lib and work the audience, and you just saw how quick and wonderful he was. I was actually managing him at the time that Hulk Hogan dropped him on his head, when he was hosting the show *Hot Properties.*

In the beginning, I used to hold auditions on Thursday afternoons at the club. And it was on one of those days that David Brenner came in. He was the first big star to perform at Catch. He had already done a bunch of Carson's. We became friends, and one Thursday he joined me for auditions, and you know yourself that some of these people can be horrible. Brenner was hysterical laughing, and he said I should take my slowest night and open the auditions to the public, which I did, and that's how it came to be on a Monday night. Monday night turned into my second busiest night other than Saturday. It was just a slam-dunk, immediate success.

When did you first hear about The Comic Strip?

I heard these guys from The Bronx were opening a club near me called The Comic Strip. Things were going so good, and I knew there was enough business for everyone. I never had a concern about it. As a matter of fact, me and a bunch of people from Catch came over here on opening night to see Billy Crystal perform. It wasn't like the days of today where you might look at it as being competitive. It never bothered me even a little. It was all new, and there was plenty of business for everybody.

So once The Comic Strip started doing well, what was the relationship between the two clubs?

I tried to blow it up about three or four times. I tried to set it on fire. I sent some goons over . . . no, we always had a good relationship. Richie and I used to call each other and ask, "Who you got hangin' around?" And if one of us needed a comic, the other one would send one over. It was always a friendly relationship.

Did you know Lucien Hold?

Very well. He was an opinionated man about what he saw, but he really had a passion for comedy and stand-ups, and I think that Richie and Bob were lucky to have him, because the comics respected him. He really had the ability, the knack, the wherewithal to put it all together and program it, to run a very tight show, and he really garnered the respect of all the comedians. Whether they liked his opinion or what he had to say was a whole other thing!

And he wouldn't forget something. He had a great memory. I live over on the West Side near the boat basin, and I would run into him from time to time. And he would always remember if I had come by The Strip to see a certain performer; he'd recall who it was months later and talk to me about that night. And I'd be astonished, like how the heck do you remember that?

Is there anything else you'd like to say about The Strip?

The Strip reminded me more of Catch, moreso than The Improv, and when I would come into the club, it was a very warm feeling because of the ambiance of the club and because of Richie and Bob as well. And I'll say a little something about Richie. Richie is a very dedicated, sweet man. Once he's a friend of yours, he's a true friend. He's a solid guy from The Bronx, and I grew up with people like that. That's why I gravitated to him. In a sense, we're kind of street people who have a certain ethic. And God bless him, he opened up The Comic Strip! So what if he copied Catch A Rising Star![25]

---

25 This particular interview turned out to be very special, because Richie had the opportunity to tell Rick that he was his "hero and his inspiration." Rick was very touched.

CHAPTER FOUR

THE NEXT GENERATION

The incredible success achieved my many of the Older Kids and Younger Kids has allowed The Comic Strip to keep it's cache of being *the* comedy club to work at if you want to become successful in the comedy world. If you can say that you passed at The Comic Strip, you'll gain automatic respect from anyone else in the business.

Most of the young comics who perform at the club now are aware of its illustrious past and are equally aware that they're on the same stage that Eddie Murphy, Jerry Seinfeld, Chris Rock, and Ray Romano performed on. If stages could only talk!

Richie and I have chosen a few of the regulars who might not be household names at the moment but are the ones we feel may be the Chris Rocks and Seinfelds of the future. Here they are, in no particular order.

Marina Franklin

Marina Franklin is known as "the sexy fairy" with good reason. She's a sexy girl without even having to try. She's also very funny and a real crowd pleaser who has appeared on *Jay Leno*, *The Chappelle Show*, *Last Comic Standing*, and *The Late, Late Show with Craig Ferguson*.

Regarding The Comic Strip, Marina says: "The Comic Strip was the first comedy club to work me, but more importantly, the first club I could call my 'home.' The Comic Strip has a more fun and functional family atmosphere than other clubs."

She recently chose to break in her one-woman show called *One Who Succeeds* at The Strip. It's the touching yet humorous story of her sister, Nailah, and how she lost her through an act of senseless violence. Marina says in her act, "Nailah got a nice African name, which means 'one who succeeds.' My name, Marina, means 'a place where you dock boats.'"

Ted Alexandro

Ted Alexandro is one of those guys who's a "comedian's comedian," meaning that anyone who appreciates the art of comedy appreciates Ted Alexandro. He has a laid-back quality to his delivery, achieved only after years and years of hard work. His comedy is sharp and clever, and he's onstage somewhere every night. He's also appeared on *Letterman*, *Comedy Central Presents*, *Conan O'Brien*, and *Louie*, and tours with Craig Ferguson.

Ted said of The Comic Strip: "For me, The Comic Strip was what it meant to be a New York comedian. When I started, I knew the history behind The Strip—names like Seinfeld, Murphy, Rock, Dennis Wolfberg, Larry Miller. You're officially a working comedian when you start working at The Strip. You're in the big leagues. That's how I felt. Then you get late sets and realize that Tuesday at 12:25 a.m. isn't quite the big leagues you imagined, so eventually you work your way up to Saturday at nine, and you're there. The Comic Strip is where I've spent twenty years learning how to become a comedian, and I'm forever grateful."

Jon Fisch

Jon Fisch is another one of those comics who just acts like he was born to be onstage. He's simply at home there. He's appeared on *Letterman*,

Last Comic Standing, Celebrity Apprentice, and on the pages of *Maxim Magazine.*

Jon is also the host of his successful podcast *In The Tank,* and he had this to say about The Strip: "The Comic Strip was the first club that I was passed at to start working in NYC. I still remember the night. I had just moved to NYC and was subletting a room in a friend's apartment near the park. I was yelling in excitement as I walked back from the club, literally screaming 'Woo-Hoo!' at the top of my lungs. I still have the scrap piece of paper Lucien gave me that night with the phone number to call in my avails. It's sitting in my wallet from that time along with the five-dollar bill I got from my first paid set at The Comic Strip."

Brian Scott McFadden

Brian Scott McFadden is a comedian/actor and a master of dialects and characters. He's been seen on *The Late Show with David Letterman* and *The Late Late Show with Craig Ferguson*, as well as in the *Ice Age* films with Ray Romano and *Robots* with Robin Williams and Halle Berry. His new CD is titled *What Women Want.*

Brian said this about The Strip: "I started doing comedy at The Comic Strip in 1947 . . . which was very difficult because the club didn't open till 1976. There was just a big hole in the ground. Stand-up comedy was very different back then. In fact, I was one of the first comics ever to actually *stand up* while doing it. Before that, comedians would usually deliver their jokes from odd crouching positions. It hurts that I am rarely given credit for this."

Nore Davis

Nore Davis's real name is Norvell Davis. Nore is a stand-up comic who was recently featured on *Russell Simmons Presents The Ruckus* on Comedy Central hosted by J. B. Smoove. Nore has also performed with and opened for Tracy Morgan, who has kind of taken Nore under his wing.

Nore said about The Strip: "I'm honored to be mentioned in the 35th Anniversary Comic Strip book. I started there eight years ago from the bottom. From open mic to bringer show to late night to a paid spot! It's an honor to be accepted, work, and learn from the most talented comedians at this club. The Comic Strip Live is my home. Period."

Pete Davidson

Pete Davidson lost his firefighter dad on 9/11. Fortunately, he was able to move past that devastating event and become a very funny comic. Now eighteen years old, he's been taken under the wing of Nick Cannon, who's been acting as Pete's mentor and who takes him on tour as his opening act. Pete is a regular on the late night show at The Comic Strip. He's also appeared on *Raw Dog Comedy* on Sirius Radio and on 92.3NOW FM radio.

He said about The Comic Strip: "Ever since I set foot in The Strip when I was sixteen years old, I dreamed of getting onstage there one day. I'm eighteen now and thanks to JR and Richie, I was given that opportunity. The Comic Strip is like a family. I've never met such a great group of people, and I feel very fortunate to be a part of it."

Jordan Rock

Jordan Rock, the youngest brother of Chris and Tony Rock, hosts late night at The Strip two nights a week and performs in clubs all over town. He also had a brief appearance on *Last Comic Standing*.

Jordan said, "I love The Strip because it allowed me to be myself, like if I didn't have an apartment I'd probably just sleep on the back bench or barber chair like I do in the afternoons. The first time I came to The Strip I did a guest spot, like March '09. I *sucked* and Richie sat me down and said, 'Hey, you're in a unique situation—you don't have to fight to make a name. You have to fight to *keep* a name," and that anytime I wanted I was welcome in The Strip. I've basically been there everyday since."

Mike Vecchione

Mike Vecchione has a very distinctive style. It's what every comic would hope to have. He's laid back and his material is cutting-edge; plus, he's nothing like what he appears to be. By his own description, he looks like a cop from Staten Island, and not a nice cop either—a nasty, racial profiling cop! Mike has been seen on TV in his own Comedy Central half-hour special, *The Tonight Show with Jay Leno*, as a semi finalist on *Last Comic Standing*, with *Russell Simmons Presents Stand-Up at the El Rey Theatre*, and Comedy Central's *Live at Gotham*, among others.

Mike said about The Strip: "The Strip is a legendary comedy club known for spawning superstars that has maintained an environment which encourages the development of young comics. I owe much of any of the success I have had to my time at The Comic Strip. Coming offstage after killing at The Comic Strip, you feel ten feet tall and bullet proof. I love The Comic Strip—there is nothing like it."

Colin Jost

Colin Jost is a senior writer on *SNL* and a talented stand-up, who was president of *Harvard Lampoon* and was featured in the New Faces show at the Just For Laughs Festival in Montreal, as well as the one in Chicago. He's also appeared on *Late Night with Jimmy Fallon* and works out regularly at The Strip.

Colin said about *The Strip*: "It's everyone's dream to have their headshot up on the wall, so twenty years from now, new comics can say, 'Hey, this guy used to be young!' Plus, it has the best food in the city, as long as you order in from The Palm."

Jay Pharoah

Jay Pharoah is a comedian and impressionist who has been a featured player on *SNL* since September 2010 and is the youngest member of the cast. He is known for his impressions of Barack Obama, Eddie Murphy, Jay-Z, and Denzel Washington, among many others, and often works out new material at The Strip. Besides *SNL,* he's been seen on *David Letterman* and has film credits in two upcoming films: *Lola Versus* with Greta Gerwig and CBS's *Get A Job,* coming out in 2013 with Brandon T. Jackson.

Jay had this to say about The Strip: "I feel honored to be able to grace the same stage as my comedy idols, Eddie Murphy and Chris Rock. It is a blessing that Richie allows me to perform longer than the light allows. I hope to one day be able to be considered a legend that generations will model themselves after and say they graced the same stage."

CHAPTER FIVE

THE LEGACY—WHAT NEXT? THE FUTURE OF THE COMIC STRIP

How do you top thirty-five years? It's a daunting task. But just because you have an illustrious history does not mean you can rest on your laurels. Every comic knows that you not only need a strong opening but you also need a killer close!

Not that The Strip needs to think about a "close" yet. It's still got a lot of life in it, and no other club in New York, or maybe even in the country, has the history of The Comic Strip. "Up and comers" still dream of performing on the same stage where Jerry Seinfeld, Eddie Murphy, and Chris Rock started out.

With that said, Richie and I have great plans for The Comic Strip in the upcoming years. It's important to Richie to leave a legacy for his children, so that if they someday want to take over the club, they can.

The Comic Strip represents a lifetime of hard work and dedication, and The Comic Strip name will live on in many ways. It's one of the reasons the lottery show is so powerful. Back in the day, there would only be two lotteries a year, and the line would be around the block. These days, we have a lottery show every Tuesday night when aspiring hopefuls get the opportunity to perform for manager J. R. and maybe even Richie and Bob. If they "pass" the lottery, they get the chance to perform on late night, which happens on Sundays, Mondays, Wednesdays, and Thursdays. It's a show that starts after the regular show ends. Comics get to do five minutes so they can develop their acts to the point where eventually they can perform on the early shows.

That five-minute set is very important, because if you ever get to the point of getting on any of the late-night television shows, that's all the time you're going to get. Every comic needs a strong five minutes.

Taking that lottery concept one step further, J. R., manager for the last fifteen years, has created an internet television show with Richie called *The Lottery Show*, where aspiring comics who want to perform at the club will audition for seasoned comics who rate them—or should I say, "be-rate" them, in front of an audience. The comments are hysterical, and you have to be strong of heart to take what is often dished out! Past judges have included Artie Lange, Tony Rock, and Patrice Oneal (one of his last appearances before he passed away). Fortunately, we tape everything that happens on that stage so it's all saved for the archives. And the show is U-Streamed internationally, which allows us to draw in a lot of visitors from abroad to our shows on a nightly basis.

We have bookers from *Letterman* stopping in on a regular basis because we attract hot new talent, and we arrange showcases for them to see who to keep an eye on.

We also recently started a new Sunday night show with a lot of the talent from *SNL*, with people like John Mulaney, and writers Colin Jost, Vanessa Bayer, and Mike O'Brien, as well as Jay Pharoah, who's become a regular at The Strip.

The Strip still has the reputation as the place to be "passed" if you want to be respected in comedy, and there's a real feeling of camaraderie among the comics who work there. The large flat-screen TVs at the bar keep crowds of comics hanging out before they go onstage and even after they get off. Schmoozing continues to be a big thing at The Strip.

Another focus of keeping the club vibrant and "hip" is through the use of marketing and social media, which has become very important to us. We now have T-shirts, mugs, water bottles, and other paraphernalia with The Comic Strip logo available for audience members to purchase after the show. We have a sizeable presence on Facebook and Twitter, and The Comic Strip website, www.comicstriplive.com, gets a large number of hits on a daily basis.

When Kevin Hart was in town and we found out he wanted to come and work out at The Strip, all we had to do was Tweet it the same afternoon, and the place was packed to overflowing. Plus, Kevin has more than 3 million of his own followers on Twitter, which has become an unbelievably powerful way of putting the word out there to the masses. Fortunately, not all 3 million of them showed up that night, because we can only accommodate 2.5 million! (And even that's pretty tight!)

Show business is about networking, and Richie and I spend a lot of time expanding our contact base so that we feel we can get to whoever we need in the comedy world. We are constantly building our relationships with well-known comics, as well as comics on the rise. I am on the comedy scene almost every night. Through my *Comedy Matters* blog and Comedy Matters TV channel, I attend many high-profile comedy events throughout the year and am always promoting The Comic Strip in everything that I do.

For example, in 2010, I co-produced an event as a benefit for Haiti starring Kevin Hart and featuring Tony Rock and Wil Sylvince. It was at the Westbury Theatre out on Long Island, and it was a sold-out, 2,800-seat event.

We had a red carpet, and Richie came out to support the cause. We did some great interviews on the red carpet, plus Richie had been Tony Rock's manager, so we also made it all about The Comic Strip. It was a great way to introduce Kevin to The Comic Strip, and once he met Richie, the guy who discovered Eddie Murphy and Chris Rock, he felt very comfortable coming in to the club to work out when he was in New York. He even recently shot an NBC interview there for Black History Month.

Whether I'm on the red carpet at the Comedy Central Roast of Donald Trump, The Friars Roast of Betty White, or at the Comedy Central Annual Comedy Awards, I'm always talking about The Comic Strip. It's that much a part of me already, and I'm proud that people associate me with the club.

We recently made a deal with the *Humor Mill Magazine*, which is based in Los Angeles, to create the *Comic Strip Radio Show* on Humor Mill Radio, which will broadcast urban comedy on a national level every week on Friday nights. Furthermore, I just launched Comedy Matters TV, based on more than 100 celebrity interviews I have shot with A-list stars, such as Jimmy Fallon, Jon Stewart, Artie Lange, Ray Romano, Chris Rock, and many others. We are planning on doing a regular Comedy Matters TV shoot from The Comic Strip, featuring interviews, new talent, and behind-the-scenes specials.

Richie is also very involved in charity work, and we plan to do more golf tournaments and charity events, like the diabetes fundraiser that Richie and I produced last year at The Strip in honor of my dad who I lost to diabetes, and with my daughter, Elizabeth DeRobertis, whose specialty as a nutritionist is working with diabetics. We are planning to make it an annual event, and Richie is connected to several charities for which he produces comedy shows and golf tournaments.

And we are looking at locations to open a sister Comic Strip in Brooklyn. Brooklyn has become the new Manhattan and is filled with young people who love comedy. They have lots of shows out there, but no real comedy club, and our plan is to fill that need. (Although neither Richie nor I have any desire to grow a Zach Galafianakis-type beard like most of the Brooklyn comics seem to favor these days!)

Richie and Bob are managing certain talent like Brian Scott McFadden and Marina Franklin, and Richie and I have plans to also manage people since I get to see so many new comedians in different venues. And the three of us are planning a documentary film as a follow-up to this book, documenting the thirty-five-year history of the club, with Chris Rock as the executive producer.

It will be very exciting for us to see who the next Seinfelds, Murphys, and Rocks are. All in all, it looks like The Comic Strip will be around for many years to come!

ACKNOWLEDGMENTS

FROM RICHIE TIENKEN:

I'd like to take this opportunity to thank all of the people who have made the last thirty-five years possible, but I'd probably need a whole other book to do that. I'd like to start by thanking my wife, Jeannie, for her love and support, as well as my kids: Dawn Marie, Chrissie, Jacqui, Richard, and Jonathan.

A lot of the people I want to thank are already in the book. I'd like to thank all of the comedians who have graced our stage since June 1, 1976, and who made The Comic Strip what it is today.

I particularly want to thank Eddie Murphy for allowing me to see a side of life that most people never get to see and for ending our relationship when he did, which allowed me to meet Jeannie and have my two boys. God works in mysterious ways, and I thank *Him* every day for all of the blessings in my life.

I want to thank Lucien, wherever he is, for his loyalty and hard work in the club for the twenty-five years he was there. Even when he was close to the end, he worked as long as he could. He was a one-of-a kind.

I want to thank JR, my current manager, for the last fifteen years, for all of his help and support, and I want to also thank the entire staff of The Strip, including Jennifer Attard, Jenn Faughnan, Tom-E Latsch, Seamus McDaid, Greg Judge, Tommy Zito, Danny O'Connor, and all of the wait staff who make the club run so smoothly. I want to thank my partner, Bob Wachs, who wants to do it all over again. He was with me at the beginning and is back again.

I'd like to thank J. L. Stermer of N. S. Bienstock for representing us with this book and for helping to make it such a spectacular project.

And I'd like to thank Skyhorse Publishing for creating a book I can be proud of.

And lastly, I'd like to thank Jeffrey Gurian, my co-author, my friend, and a talented comedian in his own right for the four years of work he put into writing this book, recording each of the interviews, and transcribing them personally to capture the essence of each of the comedians we spoke to. I couldn't have done it without him. I'd also like to thank him for bringing in J. L. Stermer, who has been great to work with.

FROM JEFFREY GURIAN:

I'd like to start by thanking all of the comedians who participated in the writing of this book, by showing up with great stories and anecdotes and allowing themselves to be open and forthcoming about their pasts and their experiences in working at The Comic Strip and with Richie Tienken.

I'd like to thank my parents, Marge and Ray Gurian, who unfortunately are not here to celebrate this book with me, but who are *always* with me in spirit, and my sister, Ronnie Muehlgay, who's always there if I need her, plus her husband Gary, and son Jonathan.

I'd like to thank my daughters, Elizabeth DeRobertis and Kathryn Siry, of whom I couldn't be prouder, and their husbands, Mike DeRobertis and Danny Siry; and their children, Nicky and Lilly DeRobertis and Brooke and Adrienne Siry.

I'd like to thank my pal Richie Tienken for giving me the opportunity to bring this book to life. When I suggested it to him back in 2008, he told me that several people over the years had proposed doing a book, and I'm honored that he trusted me to share his memories and gave me the opportunity to bring them to the world's consciousness.

He even trusted me to take the priceless, one-of-a-kind photos and other irreplaceable memorabilia from the club's walls, so I could scan them for the book. What I'm grateful to him for most is his friendship and support through this process. I don't think I could have sat in such a tiny office with anyone else for so many hours.

I'd like to thank Judith Regan for telling me I needed a powerful agent for a celeb-laden book like this, and for introducing me to Paul Fedorko and J. L. Stermer at N. S. Bienstock.

I'd like to thank J. L., in particular, for the generosity of spirit she always shows and the super amount of energy and hard work she expended to make this book as special as it is. And a special thank you to J. L.'s assistant, Samantha Bina, for all of her hard work as well.

I'd like to thank Julie Matysik from Skyhorse Publishing for believing in this book and for all of her support and hard work in seeing it to completion.

I'd like to thank JR Ravitz for his support and friendship, Seamus McDaid for getting all of the photos off the wall and out of their frames so I could scan them for the book, Tom-E for his fun spirit, Jennifer Attard for helping gather material, Jenn Faughnan for all of her help and for texting me to let me know what time to show up for late night, Bob Wachs for setting up the Billy Crystal interview, and all of the waitstaff and bartenders at The Strip who are always so friendly to me and who understand how happy it makes me to make my own drinks and squirt them into a glass using the hose by myself!

I want to thank Gladys Simon and Bob Warnick for allowing me the experience of hosting their shows at The Strip, which gave me the confidence to host late night.

And I'd like to offer up a special thank you to my Higher Power who I choose to call God, for allowing this project to come into my life and for helping me bring it to fruition. I'm very grateful for the opportunity.